FIXED BAYONETS:

A COMPLETE SYSTEM OF

FENCE FOR THE BRITISH MAGAZINE RIFLE,

EXPLAINING THE USE OF POINT, EDGES, AND BUTT,
BOTH IN OFFENCE AND DEFENCE;

COMPRISING ALSO
A GLOSSARY OF ENGLISH, FRENCH, AND ITALIAN TERMS COMMON TO
THE ART OF FENCING,

WITH A
BIBLIOGRAPHICAL LIST OF WORKS AFFECTING THE BAYONET,

BY

ALFRED HUTTON,

LATE CAPT. KING'S DRAGOON GUARDS;
AUTHOR OF 'SWORDSMANSHIP,' 'BAYONET-FENCING AND SWORD PRACTICE,'
'COLD STEEL,' ETC.

ILLUSTRATED BY J. E. BREUN.

The Naval & Military Press Ltd

published in association with

The Library & Archives Department at the Royal Armouries Museum, Leeds, specialises in the history and development of armour and weapons from earliest times to the present day. Material relating to the development of artillery and modern fortifications is held at the Royal Armouries Museum, Fort Nelson.

For further information contact:
Royal Armouries Museum, Library, Armouries Drive,
Leeds, West Yorkshire LS10 1LT
Royal Armouries, Library, Fort Nelson, Down End Road, Fareham PO17 6AN

Or visit the Museum's website at
www.armouries.org.uk

In reprinting in facsimile from the original, any imperfections are inevitably reproduced and the quality may fall short of modern type and cartographic standards.

PREFACE.

My recent work, 'Cold Steel,' has received a welcome from many of the most important journals, both English and foreign, so unexpectedly warm and generous, that I feel emboldened to lay before the public a companion to it, the matter of which I was, for various reasons, unable to include in the book itself.

The weapon I select for present discussion is our new British Magazine Rifle and its Bayonet. I add, further, what I hope may prove of interest to the fencing world — since it has hardly been attempted at all in the English language during this century — a glossary of English, French, and Italian terms of fence, together with a list of as many known treatises affecting the bayonet as I have been able to procure, in which, following the example of Gomard, I include English translations of the many foreign titles that occur therein; and I ought to add, that in compiling this latter portion of my work I am much indebted to my friend, Mr. Egerton Castle, for a large amount of valuable information and assistance.

The science of rifle shooting has — thanks to the

talent, energy, and research of the officers of our School of Musketry, at Hythe — attained such a degree of excellence and precision that it would be almost an impertinence on my part, old Musketry Instructor though I am, to offer any suggestions regarding that aspect of the Arm.

Not so, however, when it comes to be viewed in the light of hand-to-hand combat—regarded, in fact, as cold steel; here the musket and bayonet have been for years strangely neglected. A very small number of English works on the subject have from time to time appeared, but they seem to have been for the most part nipped in the bud by official frost, and so are very difficult to meet with; indeed, with the exception of Captain Anthony Gordon's 'Treatise on the Science of Defence for the Sword, Bayonet, or Pike,' 1805, which is more interesting as a curiosity than useful as a work of reference; Lieutenant (now Sir Richard) Burton's 'Complete System of Bayonet Exercise,' 1853; and my own little books, the first of which I printed at Simla in 1862, we have produced practically nothing. The American work by McClellan, 1862, we English cannot, of course, lay claim to; nor need we wish to do so, as it is confessedly not original, but a mere translation of the work of a foreign author.

On the Continent, many such works have appeared

during the present century, mainly in the first half of it—in German, French, Italian, Spanish, and even Russian—but the subject never seems to have found much favour with the teachers of the art of fence; the reason, no doubt, being that the practice weapons heretofore in use have been of a pattern so cumbersome and fatiguing as to appeal but very slightly to the fancy of the denizens of the "Salles d'Armes."

The weak point of our new weapon is its shortness as compared with its predecessors, the old muzzle-loading Enfield with its bayonet being six feet one inch in length, and the Henry-Martini being five feet seven and a half, while the present rifle with bayonet fixed, measures only five feet one; the difference in point of reach between five feet one and six feet one is obvious, and it should be noticed that certain Continental armies, notably the French, are adhering to the longer arm. As a set-off to this, however, we have, thanks to the reduced weight, a much more handy weapon, and we have, also, a more varied scope of attack, defence, and riposte. We have—first, the point; second, the two edges, to the use of which the new 'Bayonet Exercise' does not point in any way, although, be it observed, the small-bore rifle, of which I now write, must have advanced considerably further than a state of mere contemplation at the time when that somewhat meagre little manual was in process of production; and, thirdly, we have the butt, the use of which is advised, and in a measure explained, by various Continental writers, notably Gomard, Chapitre, and Chatin, and was advanced still further in 1882, by myself, in my 'Bayonet-fencing and Sword Practice,' which I brought out with the distinct purpose of furthering the views of the then Inspector and Assistant Inspector of Gymnasia, who happened to be personal friends of mine, but which the author of this same manual utterly ignores. While for the purpose of defence we have the whole length of the woodwork of the rifle from nose-cap to heel-plate, as in some cases even the butt itself may, nay more, must, be utilised for this purpose; the blade should never be so used, either according to the rules of fencing or according to the dictates of common sense, as it essentially represents the "foible," or weakest part of the weapon, and is legitimately employed solely for attack, and for attack on the person only.

Before entering upon the discussion of the management of our new arm, I shall glance critically at the Regulation Exercise recently brought into authorised use.

ALFRED HUTTON.

ARMY AND NAVY CLUB,
February, 1890.

CONTENTS.

	PAGE
CRITICAL REMARKS ON "PHYSICAL DRILL WITH ARMS, AND BAYONET EXERCISE," 1889	1
FIXED BAYONETS	13
OUR WEAPON IN ATTACK	14
OUR WEAPON IN DEFENCE	17
THE GUARD	18
THE RESTING GUARD	20
THE VOLTE	,,
CHANGE GUARD	23
THE POINT	26
THRUST	27
PRIME-THRUST	28
THROW	,,
SHORTEN ARMS	35
CHANGE OF ENGAGEMENT	36
DISENGAGEMENT AND DEROBEMENT	,,
CUT OVER	39
PARRIES AGAINST POINT	40
PARRY OF QUARTE	41
PARRY OF SIXTE	,,
PARRY OF SEPTIME	42
PARRY OF SECONDE	,,
ADVANCED LESSONS	51

FIXED BAYONETS—*continued.*

	PAGE
ATTACKS ON THE WEAPON	52
THE PRESSURE	53
THE BEAT	,,
THE FROISSEMENT	,,
THE FEINTS	54
COMPOUND RIPOSTES	59
COMBINATIONS	61

THE EDGES .. 67

THE CUTS	68
THE BUTT-THRUST	71
SUPPLEMENTARY PARRIES	72
PARRY OF PRIME	,,
PARRY OF HIGH SEPTIME	,,
PARRY OF UNDER-SIXTE	77
PARRY OF UNDER-QUARTE	78
PARRY OF HORIZONTAL PRIME	87
PARRY OF HORIZONTAL QUARTE	,,
COMBINATIONS ON THE FOREGOING LESSONS	88
MOVEMENTS WITH ADVANCED HAND	89

BUTT-FENCING .. 93

THE ATTACKS	94
GUARD	95
STROKE 1	,,
STROKE 2	96
STROKE 3	,,
STROKE 4	,,
THE THRUST	,,
THE PARRIES	,,

BUTT-FENCING—*continued*.

    COMBINATIONS OF STROKES, RIPOSTES, AND CONTRE-RIPOSTES 110

    COMBINATIONS FOR RIGHT GUARD OPPOSED TO LEFT GUARD 112

THE ASSAULT 117

BAYONET AGAINST SABRE 125

AGAINST THE LONG BAYONET 131

A GLOSSARY OF ENGLISH, FRENCH, AND ITALIAN TECHNICAL TERMS OF FENCE 133

BIBLIOGRAPHICAL LIST OF WORKS AFFECTING THE BAYONET 155

INDEX 177

ILLUSTRATIONS.

FRONTISPIECE.—PORTRAIT OF THE AUTHOR.

PLATE	PAGE
I.—THE MAGAZINE RIFLE AND BAYONET .. .. *face*	14
II.—THE GUARD	20
III.—THE THRUST	28
IV.—THE PRIME THRUST	,,
V.—THE THROW	,,
VI.—THE SHORTEN ARMS	36
VII.—THE PARRY OF QUARTE	42
VIII.—THE PARRY OF SIXTE	,,
IX.—THE PARRY OF SEPTIME	,,
X.—THE PARRY OF SECONDE	,,
XI.—THE BUTT-THRUST	68
XII.—THE PARRY OF PRIME	72
XIII.—THE PARRY OF HIGH SEPTIME	,,
XIV.—THE PARRY OF UNDER SIXTE	78
XV.—THE PARRY OF UNDER QUARTE	,,
XVI.—THE PARRY OF HORIZONTAL QUARTE	,,
XVII.—THE PARRY OF HORIZONTAL PRIME	,,
XVIII.—BUTT-FENCING. THE GUARD	96
XIX.—BUTT-FENCING. STROKE 1	,,
XX.—BUTT-FENCING. STROKE 2	,,
XXI.—BUTT-FENCING. STROKE 3	,,
XXII.—BUTT-FENCING. STROKE 4	,,
XXIII.—BUTT-FENCING. POSITION IN PARRYING STROKES 3 AND 4 WITH SIXTE AND CENTRE-SIXTE ..	,,

CRITICAL REMARKS ON 'PHYSICAL DRILL WITH ARMS, AND BAYONET EXERCISE,' 1889.

THE first four practices of "Physical Drill" form, undoubtedly, an admirable substitute for the tiresome "Extension Motions" of the days of our youth, and the author has developed them in a manner deserving of hearty commendation, although he can hardly be credited with originality of conception, as an exercise with the musket very similar to this was in vogue at Mr. Angelo's School of Arms upwards of thirty years ago. I learned it there myself, and very useful I found it. But when we come to the fifth practice (p. 8), which forms a kind of introduction to the new Bayonet Exercise, there is much to be found in which it is impossible for any person possessing true knowledge of the art of fence to concur with him.

It is to be presumed that the object of this part of the work is to impart to the soldier facility in the management of his weapon as a practical arm, and not as a parade-ground plaything; and it is clear to me that certain details introduced here by our author, but traceable through the Bayonet Exercise of 1885 to the older exercises of Angelo, which must be the inevitable cause of cramped action, are in no way conducive to this end. In justice to the memory of Angelo, however, it ought to be remembered that his work was written for the barrack-yard only, and was "by no means intended for a system of Bayonet-fencing such as is occasionally practised by foreign troops."

The regulation exercise of 1889, which I have now before me, orders that the "Engage" (pp. 8 and 9) shall be formed with "*the right hand holding the small firmly against the hip*," a posture pretty certain to engender a rigidity of muscle, which was all very well in the attitude of "Charge Bayonets" of the drill-masters of the last century, when the weapon was regarded purely as an "arme de choc," but which is fatal when introduced into an exercise in which flexibility of limb and celerity of movement form the main essential of the soldier's efficiency.

. I now turn to the "Points" (p. 9):—The "First Point" follows so entirely the line of Angelo and his predecessors that there is no need to make any further mention of it. But with regard to the "Second Point" (p. 9), generally recognised as the "throw," in which the left hand is made to quit the rifle altogether, it is vastly different. This the writer seems to regard as an invention of his own; and a part of it, to which I shall have to draw special attention, most undoubtedly is so. I knew, however, a throw point of somewhat similar nature, which was in constant use at the Aldershot Gymnasium, twenty years ago; it was the same as that mentioned by Angelo in his 'Bayonet Exercise' (p. 22), where he speaks of it as follows:—"It must be borne in mind, however, that great caution and care must be used when so delivering a thrust direct to the front, as the assailant is likely to be disarmed, or his musket so thrown out of the line of defence as not to be easily recovered; in fact, such a thrust should only be resorted to when there is every chance of its being given effectually, and having the left hand quite prepared to resume its hold."

This "throw point" I never quite agreed with, and in my first treatise, 'Swordsmanship,' I omitted it altogether. I found from experience that most men, not excepting myself, were but too much inclined to let go with the left hand in making a thrust, with the view of obtaining a little more reach; and this tendency being, as Angelo has shown, a very dangerous one, it should be repressed as much as possible, and certainly should not be made a compulsory part of the soldier's education. I afterwards, in 1868, introduced a modification of the "throw" into the K. D. G. School, and included it also in my 'Bayonet-fencing and Sword Practice' of 1882; and in this modification I find that the treatise of M. Gomard, which I had not then met with, bears me out.

The old-fashioned "throw," it is seen, surrenders control over the weapon in a very inconvenient fashion, but the new Bayonet Exercise carries the fault still further; it actually compels the poor soldier, after having completely quitted his rifle with his advanced hand, *to therewith* "*grasp* (sic) *his thigh about midway*," thereby making it doubly difficult for him to regain that hold of his weapon about which Henry Angelo, a master of European reputation, speaks so emphatically. Can, I ask, the gentleman who has introduced this ridiculous movement, or can the higher authorities who have forced it upon our men, give any sane reason for having done so? It certainly cannot increase either the rapidity or the accuracy of the thrust, while it as certainly precludes a recovery speedy enough to parry a prompt riposte. It is worse than silly to make a man learn in a fencing lesson, for such this bayonet drill is supposed to be, that which would be absolutely dangerous to him in a fight with sharps; the thing can be nothing more than a trick of the parade ground, intended, not to enhance individual skill, but to produce mere uniformity in point of performance, and so deceive the eye of non-experts by giving the exercise a smarter and more brilliant appearance than an elementary fencing lesson usually presents.

With regard to the "Third Point" (p. 9), it is an innovation certainly differing from Angelo's "Shorten Arms," for which it has been made a substitute. Various ways of effecting this "bras raccourci" thrust have been recommended by the great Continental writers, and they certainly may each and all be of some use in a *melée*, but the introducer of this new one has somewhat exaggerated notions of its efficacy in a combat with a dismounted swordsman. On page 26 it is stated with regard to this "Third Point," that it is useful "when a swordsman on foot succeeds in getting into too close quarters." This statement does not bear close examination; the swordsman, be it observed, has already succeeded in advancing "within measure," and his attack must necessarily be quicker that that of the bayoneteer, and that solely by reason of the position here enforced, as, on referring to Plate M, we find the point elevated and directed in a line which would pass well over the opponent's head, while the left hand has been shifted so as to grasp the rifle close to the muzzle; the swordsman, therefore, requires but *one* movement, the forward one, to complete his attack, while it will take *two* movements to effect the same with the bayonet—the first to bring the point into line, and the second to drive the thrust home. Again, from the fact of the point being held high, it is perfectly easy for the swordsman to dominate or command it from below, as I have already demonstrated in 'Cold Steel,' in the chapter devoted to sabre against bayonet; and, further, the author has entirely overlooked the exposed position of the advanced hand, so much so that he has made either the destruction of that hand, or the commanding of the weapon with a view to other and more drastic measures, a mere matter of choice for the sabreur. In fact, his boasted "Third Point," instead of being a safeguard to the bayoneteer, is a source of positive danger.

The "Change Arms" appears to be a somewhat cumbersome proceeding, in place of which I think I can suggest something more rapid as my work proceeds; it is of course intended to place the men in the position of left-handed fencers, as was Angelo's "About," which gave an instantaneous change of front as well as change of guard, in case of a sudden attack in rear.

The Lunge (p. 10) is much advocated in this new system, in conjunction with all three points, on the plea that it gives increase of reach, which is certainly the case; but this advantage is more than balanced by the difficulty of recovering to the second position; it must be noted that, firstly, the weapon is a heavy one, and secondly, it is propelled forward "*to the full extent of both arms,*" the men being ordered also to "*lean well forward, by straightening the right leg,*" the momentum of which, even in the case of the simple "First Point," has an unavoidable tendency to drag the trunk still further forward into an overbalanced posture, and when to this is superadded the increased momentum caused by the lunge—and recollect that the lunge here ordered is a full one—this liability to overbalance is materially increased, and the evil is enhanced still further when the lunge is combined with the "throw" point, and its absurd accompaniment of letting go the rifle and grasping the thigh with the left hand. I grant, however, that the lunge is admissible in certain cases when engaged with a mounted man.

I do not deny that some very strong and active men can be trained to perform these lunges with a fair degree of skill, and we have seen such an exhibition at the Royal Military Tournament; but we must remember that these were picked men, and scarcely a fair sample of the average rank and file.

The Guards.—Here the writer (p. 16) has curiously fallen into the same error which I myself committed in my earlier works on these subjects, that of confusing the two terms "Guard" and "Parry," to correct which I devoted some little space in 'Cold Steel.'

In forming the first and second of these "guards" (p. 17), he lays down peremptorily that "*the right hand and forearm are to remain firm at the side, the defence being entirely formed by the left hand moving the rifle to the right or left without relaxing its grasp, as a lever, the right hand being the fulcrum.*" Here the writer has tumbled into an error worse than any of those which made the supersession of Angelo's Bayonet Exercise necessary, as at any rate that master does not insist on making the right hand and forearm a positive fixture such as we have here. Here we have again that cramped position which I have already complained of in the "Engage," only in the present case the rigidity is likely to become much more pronounced, and to develop a tendency to allow the *body* to be swung sideways, influenced by the action of the left arm, so that the "fulcrum," of which this gentleman talks so learnedly, will not be "the right hand and forearm," but the very *pelvis* itself instead; he ignores, in fact, one of the leading principles of all sound fencing, namely, that all parrying movements shall be made with the arms only, and especially without disturbing the position of the body.

A further and still grosser blunder (p. 16) does he commit by ordering these two "guards" to be formed by *passing the muzzle a few inches to the right or left*, and so of course deflecting the point of the bayonet off the line to a still greater degree, and in the case of weapons of point only, such as this one is, this deviation from the direct line has been regarded, and rightly so, as a "damnable heresy," from the days of the semi-mythical Pietro Moncio to the present hour; this lateral movement leads us to suppose, moreover, that the writer intends to make the men parry with the blade, which is in fact the "foible"—an idea quite as heterodox, and quite as impracticable as the other which I have condemned.

Touching the "Third Guard" (p. 16) the order that *both elbows should be kept close to the body* seems to tend again to produce that element of stiffness concerning which I have had to say so much already; further, in forming it, the soldier is commanded to "*lower the point, by passing the rifle in a circular motion downwards to the right.*" If this order is faithfully obeyed, the circular movement will naturally be to the right, and altogether wide of the body, leaving the whole of it exposed to attack; laid down as it is, it parries absolutely nothing. The illustration, however (Plate S), has a practical look; it fairly represents the "Third Guard" of an exercise of my own, which the authorities of the Gymnasium at Aldershot made use of for some twenty years; it defended the low inner line, and I shall introduce it again in the ensuing pages, under the more technical name of "Septime."

The writer, throughout the whole of his Bayonet Exercise, seems unable to divest himself of the old-fashioned barrack-yard notions of buckram rigidity—we are so often confronted with his constricted attitude of the right hand and arm; for even in effecting the Beat (p. 22), an attack on the blade intended to force an opening, he as usual compels the soldier to keep "*the right hand firm against the side.*" In such a posture the lateral beat alone can be made, and that but clumsily, while the much more decisive "froissement," as well as the "coulement," is rendered an absolute impossibility.

There are some other minor matters to which I might take exception, but to criticise them too severely might seem ungracious; I may, however, have to advert to them as the further portion of my work proceeds.

FIXED BAYONETS.

FIXED BAYONETS.

In "Fixed Bayonets" I shall follow mainly the lines of my former work, 'Bayonet-fencing and Sword-practice,' from which I see no reason to deviate excepting in regard to some minor details which the alteration in the form of the weapon renders necessary. I have made, of course, considerable additions, and I have further, where necessary, borrowed slightly from earlier foreign works.

I am alive to the fact that my first efforts at going into the question of Bayonet-fencing were very incomplete, they being written chiefly for the guidance of the teachers of certain Regimental Clubs and Schools, such as the "Cameron Fencing Club" of the 79th Highlanders, as it existed in 1862, whose instructors I was obliged to train entirely myself, there being no one else capable of doing it; this, too, was at an out of the way up-country station in India, where such things as works of reference were utterly beyond my reach. Now, however, that a higher class of arm has been provided for our soldiers, it may be well to introduce to the public a more comprehensive scheme for its use than has hitherto found its way into print in our language.

I shall first consider our bayoneteer as contending against an adversary armed similarly to himself, and secondly, bearing in mind the weak point of our weapon—its shortness—I shall glance at its employment against one of superior length.

Our Weapon in Attack.

We must now examine our arm to ascertain its offensive powers. Here we have three great factors of attack. Of these, the *Point* of course takes the first place, as being the most deadly as well as the most rapid form of attack that can be delivered. Secondly come the *Edges*, of which we have two, corresponding to those of the sabre, namely, the *true edge*, which is inclined downwards and away from the muzzle, and the *false edge*, which lies upwards and is nearest to the muzzle. These edges are useful mostly for the purpose of riposte, but they may be employed in initial attack under circumstances which I shall hereafter describe.

Thirdly we have the *Butt*, the use of which has, as I have remarked before, been suggested by several Continental writers; but none of them, so far as I

PLATE I.

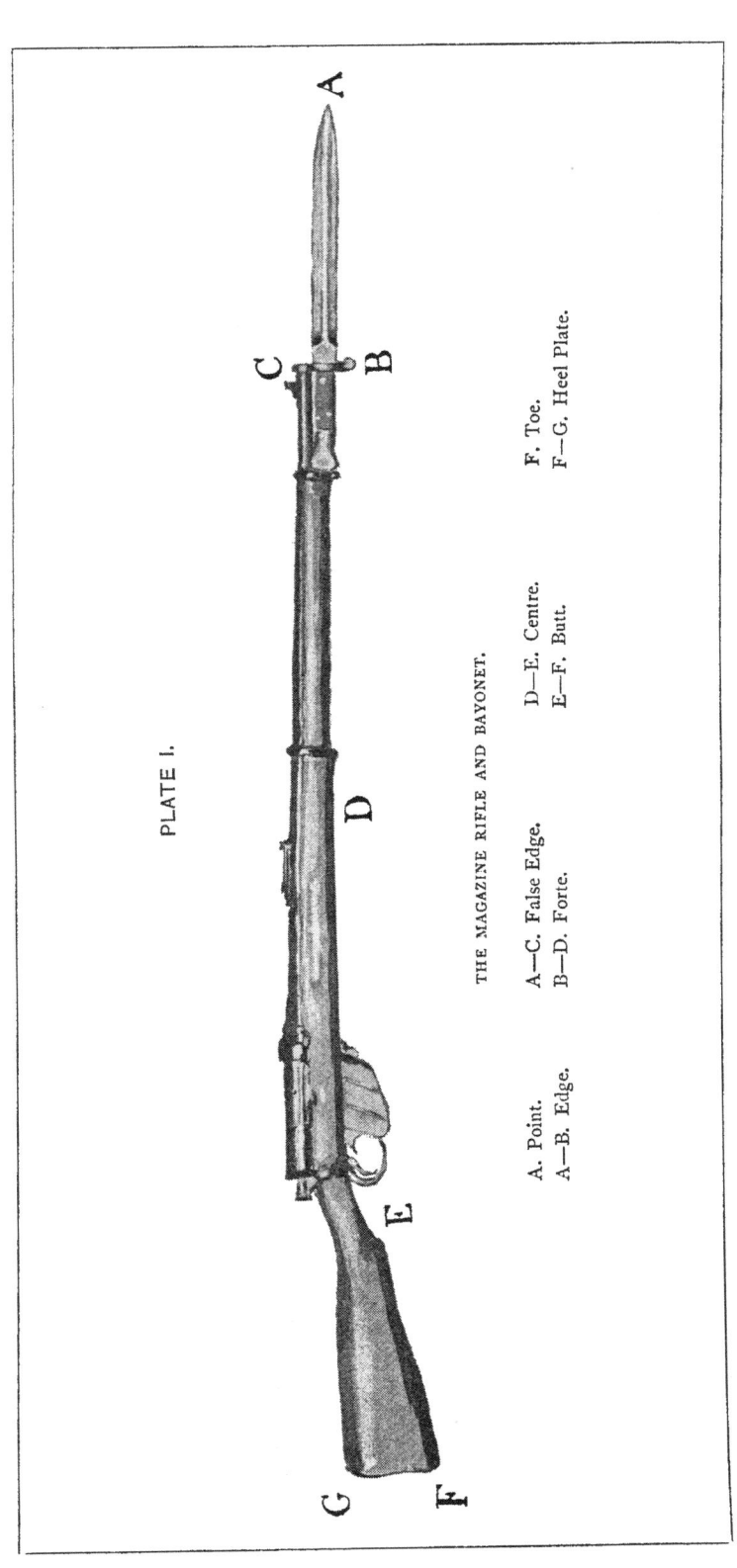

THE MAGAZINE RIFLE AND BAYONET.

A. Point.
A—B. Edge.
A—C. False Edge.
B—D. Forte.
D—E. Centre.
E—F. Butt.
F. Toe.
F—G. Heel Plate.

have been able to gain access to their works, seem to have reduced it to any set form of what I must undertake to christen "Butt-fencing." It is useful occasionally in riposte, when it takes the place of the edge, but it is applicable chiefly to the position known as "Corps à corps," when the combatants are so close together that it is impossible for either of them to disentangle his weapon or withdraw his point; it can also be employed against the enclosing of a resolute swordsman, and in such case I think it is preferable to any kind of "Shorten Arms," being much quicker, much more unexpected, and quite as conclusive in the effect of its blow; it should, moreover, be extremely useful in a melée or in a crowd, when troops have been called out to clear the streets, when, naturally, it is advisable not, if possible, to have recourse to the absolutely deadly bayonet itself.

Our Weapon in Defence.

Next we must consider our weapon in its defensive aspect, and we must observe that it presents three great factors of defence. The blade, being the "foible," must never be so used. The first is that part of the stock which lies between the muzzle and the "balance," the part, that is, which rests in the advanced hand; it corresponds to the

c

"Forte" of the sword, and by that name I shall call it; with this part the attacks of point are usually parried. The second is the "Centre," the part between the balance and the small—the part, in fact, between the two hands—and with it are parried certain ripostes of point, some of the cuts, and most of the strokes of the butt. The third is the "Butt," which parries both thrusts and cuts directed at the lower lines.

The Guard.

I must again call the attention of the reader to the necessity of avoiding any confusion between the two terms, "Guard" and "Parry," the latter being a distinctly defensive movement, while the former, the guard, is simply that posture which is at once the most ready for attack and the most secure for defence.

The feet should now assume a position similar to that used on guard in sabre play, excepting that the left foot should be in advance; they should be placed well apart, the average distance between them being about twenty-four inches, but this must be regulated in conformity to the height of the man, the knees being well but not too much bent, so as to be supple and ready for movement in any direction; the body upright but not stiff, and its weight equally distributed between the legs, so that there should be no more strain on one than on the other.

The left hand should hold the rifle just in front of the backsight (the backsight itself is placed exactly at the "balance," and it is an awkward thing to take hold of), the right hand of course grasping the small, and the point of the bayonet in line with the opponent's face.

Teachers and pupils must never forget that elasticity of limb is the main essential to success in wielding the bayonet, and the greatest care must be taken to avoid anything which may tend to cause rigidity; the hands, therefore, must *hold the weapon somewhat lightly*, a tight grip with the hands invariably causes stiffness in the wrists and arms.

The rifle should rest easily in the left hand, with the true edge in line with the centre knuckles, as a sabre is held, and in a medium guard, that is to say, not covering directly either outside or inside, but ready to parry promptly in any direction. When the bayonets are engaged on the inside the guard will be a Quarte Medium, and when on the outside a Sixte Medium.

I do not approve of engaging in a Quarte Guard with "opposition," as Chapitre recommends, because in such a position a very wide opening is shown on the outside in the region of the advanced forearm, which can be easily reached with a disengagement, and it is impossible to follow this movement with a circular parry as is done in foil practice ; the only parries practicable with the bayonet are the simple ones, and these are the most easily effected from this Medium Guard.

The Resting Guard.

Draw back the hands a little, and lower the rifle until the right hand rests on the upper part of the right thigh, and the back of the left hand and wrist on the left thigh ; the point of the bayonet is now directed a little low, and slightly off the line to the left, but it must be remembered that this guard, like the " Resting Medium " in 'Cold Steel' is only applicable when the opponent is out of reach, and its object is to afford repose to the muscles in order that they may be the more ready for active operations when fighting distance has been gained.

The Volte.

This must not be confounded with the old-fashioned movement so named in small-sword fencing, which was designed to remove the body from the direct line, and so avoid a sword thrust; the Volte I propose, which is nearly that of Chapitre, is intended simply to effect a change of front in order to face a rapid " traverse " on the part of the opponent, or to meet any other sudden flank attack. It is executed as follows :—

PLATE II.

THE GUARD.

To the Right—Volte. Turn to the right on the toes of the advanced foot, describing a quarter circle backwards with the rearward foot from right to left, which will bring it behind the other again in the position of " Guard."

To the Left—Volte. Turn to the left on the toes of the advanced foot, describing a quarter circle backwards from left to right, and bring it to the position of " Guard."

These movements effect an immediate change of front to right or left, without in any way disarranging the position of body or weapon.

CHANGE GUARD.

This, I think, is a more appropriate name for the movement than that of " Change Arms," and certainly it is a quicker mode of reversing the position of Guard from right hand to left hand than is the " Change Arms" ordered in the authorised manual of 1889, whether employed in the set lesson or in loose play; I deduce it from my changes between the Quarte and Tierce Guards of the " Great Stick " exercises in ' Cold Steel.' These changes are effected on the move, either advancing or retiring.

CHANGE GUARD (FROM RIGHT TO LEFT) RETIRING.

Turn on the toes of the right foot, using them as a pivot, and retire the left foot about twenty-four inches behind it ; the right toe will now point to the front and the left toe to the left. At the same time extend the arms, with the rifle in a horizontal position, sufficiently to allow the heelplate to be quite clear of the body, and pass it across to the left side without shifting the hands, the right hand passing underneath the left forearm ; then seize the balance with the right hand, and the small with the left. We have thus assumed the "Guard" for the left-handed lessons or play, which in every way corresponds to the ordinary "Guard" we have just quitted, and which we may name the *Left Guard*.

CHANGE GUARD (FROM LEFT TO RIGHT) RETIRING.

Turn on the toes of the left foot, and bring the right foot behind it, the left toe pointing to the front and the right toe to the right ; extend the arms as before, and pass the rifle across to the right side, the left hand passing under the right forearm, seize the balance with the left hand, and the small with the right. You are now in the position of the original Guard

CHANGE GUARD (FROM RIGHT TO LEFT) ADVANCING.

Turn on the toes of the left foot, bringing the right foot forward in front of it, passing the rifle to the left as before, and come to Left Guard.

CHANGE GUARD (FROM LEFT TO RIGHT) ADVANCING.

Turn on the toes of the right foot, bring the left foot forward in front of it, pass the rifle across to the right, and come to Guard.

It is a pity that the military authorities should have abolished the "About" of Angelo's Exercise, which was done by turning to the rear on the heels without moving off the ground, changing the hold of the musket, and assuming the changed Guard facing to the rear. This movement, although not applicable in a set lesson, might be of infinite service in a melée.

The movements of Advancing, Retiring, Traversing, Timing, Passing, &c., are all fully explained in 'Cold Steel,' and therefore a repetition of them here would be superfluous.

THE POINT.

The lessons should now be given individually, the master having the entire front of his body protected by a stout plastron.

The bayonet, when regarded as a weapon pointed only, must be recognised as, as it were, a two-handed small sword, and thus it must be subject to rules of a somewhat similar description, and in wielding it both hands must share in the work of its manipulation, as in the Great Stick Play, and neither hand should ever be used exclusively as "lever" or "fulcrum" as the writer of the Bayonet Exercise of 1889 has laid down.

We have now to observe the four divisions of the body, or lines of attack, as they appear when on Guard.

First, the *Upper Inside*, which corresponds to the Quarte line of foil fencing; and is on the right of the rifle above the hands.

Second, the *Upper Outside* or "Sixte" line, on the left of the rifle, above the hands.

Third, the *Low Inside* or "Septime" line, on the right of the rifle, below the hands.

Fourth, the *Low Outside* or "Seconde" line, on the left of the rifle, below the hands.

The attack, whether with point or edge, should always be made with the "allonge," or extension, and *never*, except at a mounted man, with the "developpement" or full lunge, on account of the tendency to loss of balance, which, with a hastate weapon the full lunge always entails.

In bayonet fencing there are five thrusts, namely, the Thrust, the Prime-thrust, the Throw, the Full Throw, and the Shorten Arms, which I will explain in the following lesson:—

On Guard. Fall back, by retiring the right foot, to the position of Guard, as above described.

Prove Distance. Extend the rifle, until the point touches the right breast of the master.

The weapons must now be crossed in the Quarte Medium, the point of juncture being just below the Cross Guard.

Thrust. Advance the rifle smartly in a horizontal position, above the height of the shoulder, barrel uppermost, to the full extent that the arms will allow, until the point strikes the breast of the master on the upper inside line, at the same time completing the extension by bracing the right knee.

Guard.	Withdraw the point, and come to Guard.
Prime-thrust.	Raise the rifle, sling uppermost, the butt and right hand to be as high as the right ear, and the back of the hand towards it.
Two.	Deliver the thrust, with the sling still uppermost, at the upper inside line.
Guard.	Withdraw the point, and come to Guard.
Throw.	Advance the point as far as the extension will permit, *opening the advanced hand, and allowing the rifle to glide over the palm of it*, striking the breast of the master on the upper inside line; the left hand will now be against the trigger guard, and must not be moved from its position, but must be ready to resume its proper hold instantly on the completion of the thrust, or in the event of the thrust being parried.
Guard.	Withdraw the point, and come to Guard.

The "throw" here recommended is the same as the " Glissé de l'Arme" of Gomard and Chatin, and against an opponent on foot it is the only real safe

PLATE III.

THE THRUST.

PLATE IV.

THE PRIME-THRUST.

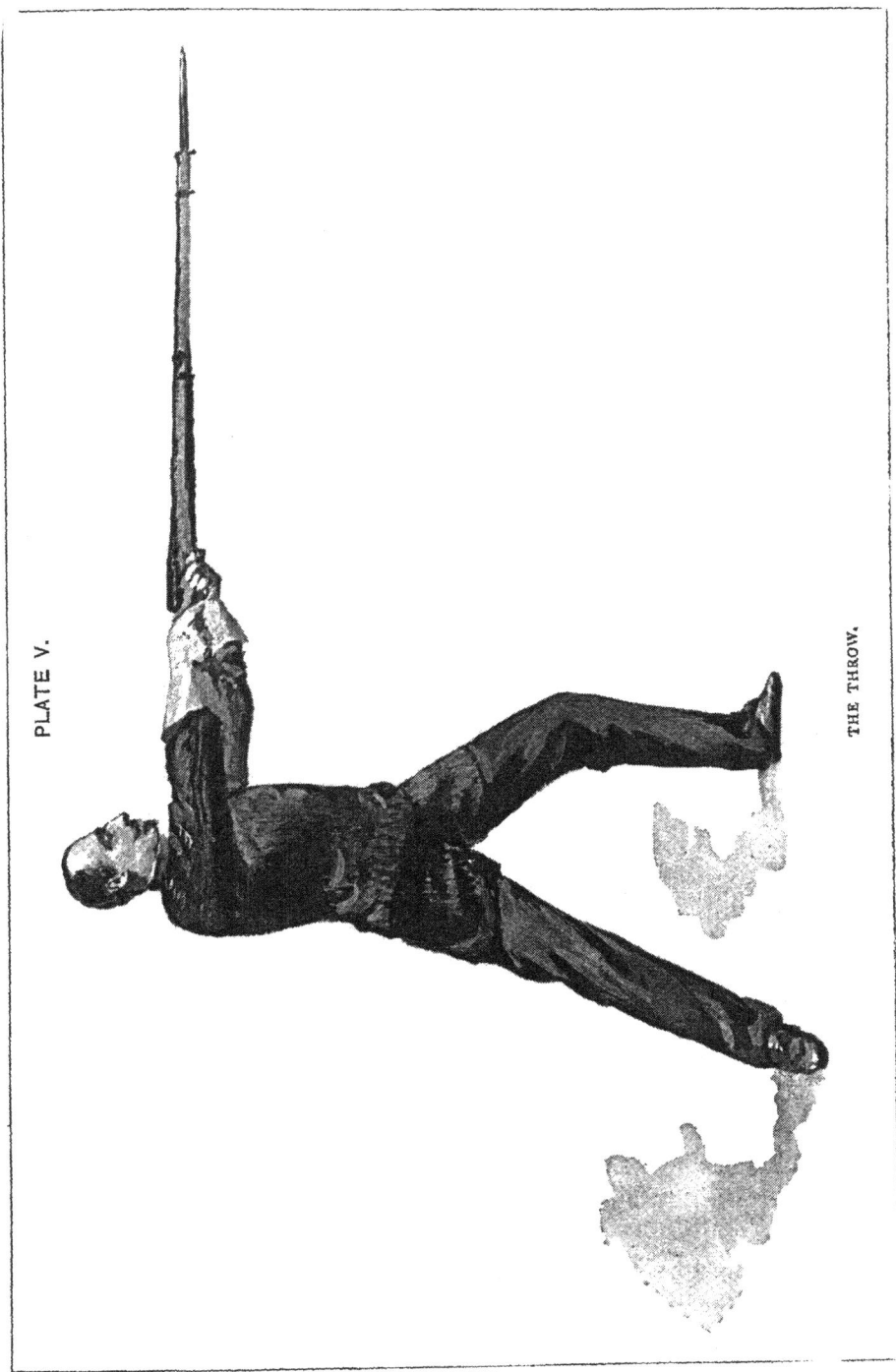

PLATE V.

THE THROW.

one; it should be, however, but sparingly used; while the full throw, as mentioned by Angelo, and known to the earlier writers as " jet de l'arme," " coup lancé," or " coup lâché," in which the left hand quits the rifle altogether, should be reserved for use against a mounted man.

The absolute necessity of keeping the left hand immediately underneath the rifle in effecting the " throw," ought to be thoroughly impressed on the pupil; my experience with bayonet-fencing, which extends over more than thirty years, shows me that men are *naturally* too much inclined to let go altogether with the advanced hand, so that extra care should be taken to correct the tendency.

Shorten Arms. Bring the rifle down to a horizontal position, with the point direct to the front, carry it back to the full reach of the arms, and about level with the waist, the barrel to rest on the left forearm; and brace the left knee.

Thrust. Deliver the point as before.

The Shorten Arms partakes to a certain extent of the nature of a " guard," it being the position best adapted for giving point at an enemy who has advanced within measure; the attitude of the arms is less stiff than that of Angelo, who, according to his illustration, with which his letterpress does not entirely accord, shows the arms and the musket at the height of the shoulder.

Change of Engagement, or of Line.

This is a new engagement, formed on the opposite line by dipping the point underneath and close to the opponent's weapon, and joining it again on the other side.

Disengagement and Derobement.

These two movements are closely allied, in fact it is only of late years that the distinction has been recognised; the purpose of both is to take advantage of some opening for attack shown in a line other than that of the present engagement.

The *Disengagement* is an attack made by changing laterally, that is, from inside to outside or the reverse, by passing the point underneath and as close as possible to the opponent's *forte*, following instantly with a straight thrust in the opposite line.

The *Derobement* is made by changing from the upper to the lower line, and *vice versâ*, when that line happens to be covered, following immediately with a straight thrust.

PLATE VI.

THE SHORTEN ARMS.

To these I shall call further attention after the lessons of parries against point.

Cut Over.

Raise the bayonet and pass it over the opponent's point, directing the thrust at the high line on the opposite side; this can only be done when the opponent's point is a little high.

When all these thrusts have been well learned, the master must give the order " Change Guard," when the lesson will be performed from the left guard.

PARRIES AGAINST POINT.

As there are four lines of attack with the point, so there are, according to all the received rules of the Art of Fencing, at least four simple defences or parries, that is to say, one for each line; their names are:—

Quarte, which defends the high inside line.
Sixte, which defends the high outside line.
Septime, which defends the low inside line.
Seconde, which defends the low outside line.

In forming these parries, I adhere mainly to the instructions contained in my former work, 'Bayonet-fencing and Sword practice.' In their execution, care must be taken to ensure the greatest possible flexibility of the limbs, especially of the arms and shoulders.

It scarcely need be explained that in all parries, whether against a thrust or a blow, the attack must be received on the woodwork of the rifle, and never on the barrel.

To carry out the lessons of the parries, I place the master (*M.*) and the pupil (*P.*) opposite to each other, proceeding with the instruction as I did in 'Cold Steel.' They will engage, crossing their weapons in a quarte medium.

M.	*P.*
Thrust (at the upper inside line).	*Parry Quarte*, by passing the rifle slightly to the right, and so causing the opponent's weapon to glide off the *forte;* the point of the bayonet must not be allowed to deviate from the direction of the opponent's face.
	On Guard.
Disengage and thrust (at the upper outside line).	*Parry Sixte*, by passing the rifle a little to the left, turning the edge just enough to the left to allow the woodwork to meet the opponent's blade, by allowing the rifle to revolve in the left hand, and making a light springy beat on the opponent's weapon near the point, taking care to recover instantly from any deviation of the point from the direct line.
	On Guard.

M.	*P.*
Derobe and thrust (at the low inside line).	*Parry Septime*, by lowering the point, and passing the rifle slightly to the right, the point to be kept in line with the opponent; this will parry a thrust at the low inside line, or will arrest a disengagement.
	On Guard.
Engage in Sixte Medium.	
Derobe and thrust (at the low outside).	*Parry Seconde*, by lowering the point, turning the sling up, and carrying the rifle a little to the left, making a slight beat on the opponent's weapon, as in the parry of sixte.
	On Guard.

These parries must also be practised from the left guard.

PLATE VII.

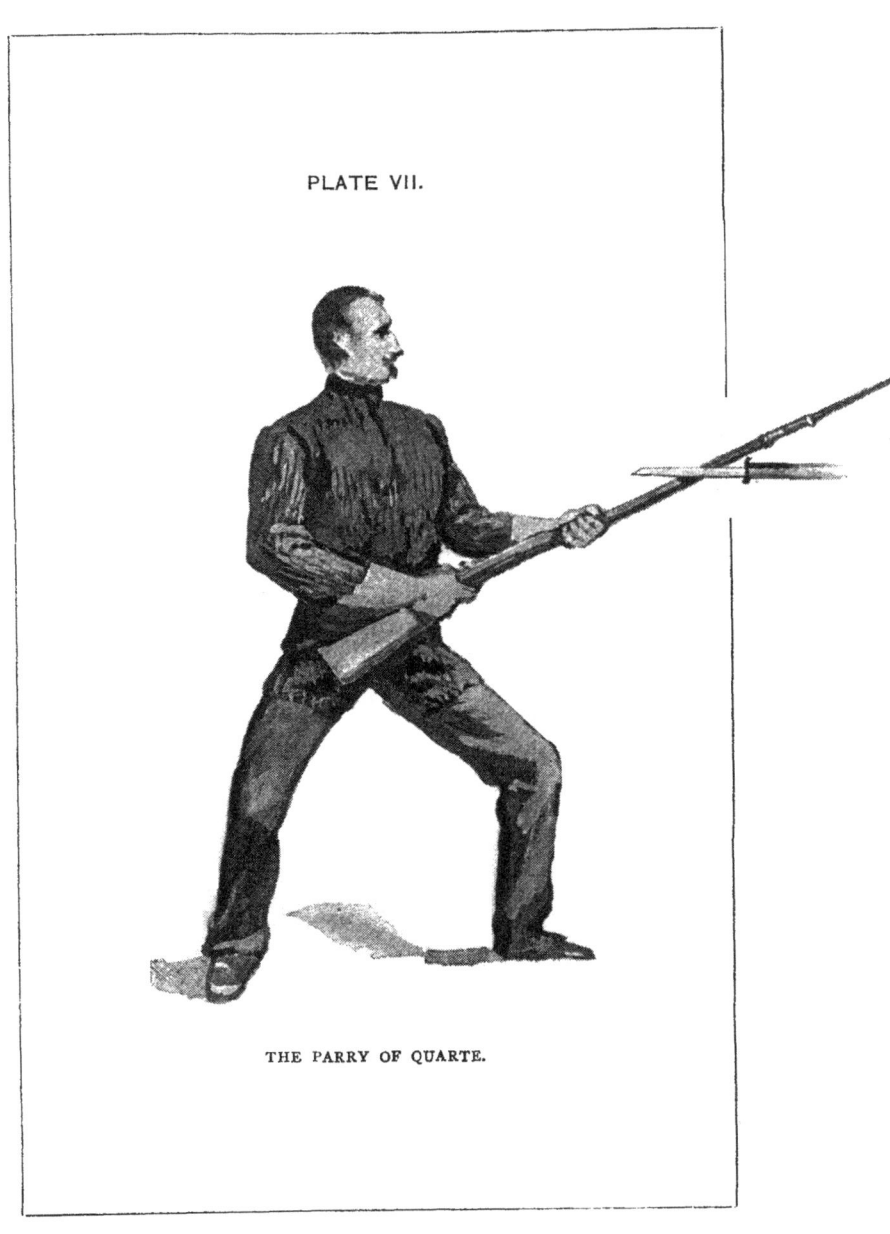

THE PARRY OF QUARTE.

PLATE VIII.

THE PARRY OF SIXTE.

PLATE IX.

THE PARRY OF SEPTIME.

PLATE X.

THE PARRY OF SECONDE.

ADVANCED LESSONS.

SIMPLE ATTACKS AND THEIR PARRIES, WITH ONE RIPOSTE.

WHEN the riposte is executed by the pupil the master should usually allow himself to be touched, but when he himself makes it he should be very careful to cause the pupil to form the proper parry.

Engage in Quarte Medium.

M.	*P.*
Thrust.	Parry quarte, derobe, and thrust low.
Parry septime.	
	On Guard.

When the pupil performs this in a satisfactory manner the lesson must be reversed, when *P.* will commence.

Derobe and thrust low.	Parry septime, thrust high.
Parry quarte.	
	On Guard.

Reverse the lesson.

Disengage and thrust.	Parry sixte, thrust high.
Parry sixte.	
	On Guard.

Reverse the lesson.

M.	*P.*
Disengage and thrust.	Parry sixte, derobe, and thrust low.
Parry seconde.	
	On Guard.

Reverse the lesson.

Cut over and thrust.	Parry sixte, disengage, and thrust.
Parry quarte.	
	On Guard.

Reverse the lesson.

Engage in Sixte Medium.

Cut over and thrust.	Parry quarte, derobe, and thrust.
Parry septime.	
	On Guard.

Reverse the lesson.

These lessons should be practised also on the Left Guard.

Attacks on the Weapon.

Of the various movements of this class used in foil-fencing there are but three which I consider applicable to the bayonet. Their object is, primarily, to gain an opening by force; and, secondly, as feints employed in conjunction with some other movement to effect it by strategy. They are named the Pressure (*pression*), the Beat, or Dry Beat (*battement sec*.), and another kind of beat known in French as "Froissement"—a term for which we have no satisfactory equivalent in English, so I must perforce adhere to the French name, which I have already had to do with regard to the "Derobement."

The Pressure.

The weapons being joined in quarte or sixte medium, press slightly with the woodwork of your own rifle upon the opponent's blade or foible, and as his point deviates from the line deliver a straight thrust.

The Beat.

The Beat, or "Dry" Beat, is a purely lateral movement, it is effected by giving a smart springy rap to the opponent's blade or foible in order to drive his point out of line; it is followed, of course, by a direct thrust at the opening thus made.

The Froissement.

This movement, of the nature of the Beat and also of the Pressure, assisted by a movement in the form of a "Coulé," is effected by striking the opponent's weapon sharply with a downward gliding motion. It is much more forcible than the "dry" beat; it must be followed instantly by the direct thrust.

In all these attacks on the weapon, care must be taken that the point does not deviate from the direct line.

The Feints.

In my earlier book, 'Swordsmanship and Bayonet-fencing,' I recommended that in effecting the feints the point should be gradually advanced, so that the feint and the real attack should be, so to speak, one continuous movement. In those days this was in common use, but, as far as the foil is concerned, it has now become obsolete: it is, however, still applicable to the bayonet, especially in a system which does not recognise the lunge. The most useful feints are the following:—

Engage in Quarte Medium.

Feint a straight thrust and disengage (to deceive quarte).	Advance the point slightly to make me think that you intend a straight thrust, and as I parry quarte, disengage and send the thrust home in the opposite line.

Feint a thrust and dérobe (to deceive quarte).	Feint a thrust as before, and on my parry of quarte drop the point to the lower line and thrust home.
One two (to deceive sixte).	Disengage, advancing the point a little, and on my parry of sixte disengage back again and thrust in the quarte line.
Under and over (to deceive septime).	Feint a low thrust, and on my parry of septime deliver the point high.
Thrust, and one two (to deceive quarte and sixte).	Feint a thrust, I parry quarte; deceive it by disengaging, on which I parry sixte; disengage again, and thrust home in the quarte line.
One two three (to deceive sixte and quarte).	Disengage, I parry sixte; disengage again, I parry quarte; deceive it by disengaging a third time, and thrust home in the sixte line.

Change to Sixte Medium.

Thrust and disengage (to deceive sixte). — Feint a direct thrust, and as I parry sixte, disengage and thrust home in the quarte line.

Thrust and derobe (to deceive sixte). — Feint a direct thrust, and as I parry sixte, drop the point and thrust home in the low outside line.

One two (to deceive quarte). — Disengage, and as I parry quarte, deceive it by disengaging again, and thrusting home in the quarte line.

Under and over (to deceive seconde). — Feint at low line, and as I drop my point to parry, derobe and thrust home in the high line.

Thrust and one two (to deceive sixte and quarte). — Feint a thrust, I parry sixte; disengage, I parry quarte; deceive it and thrust home in the sixte line.

One two three (to deceive quarte and sixte.) — Disengage, I parry quarte; disengage again, I parry sixte; deceive it, and thrust home in the quarte line.

Engage in Quarte Medium.

Cut over and disengage (to deceive sixte).
Pass your bayonet over my point, I parry sixte; deceive it by disengaging and thrusting home in the quarte line.

Cut over and derobe (to deceive sixte).
Pass your bayonet over my point, I parry sixte; deceive it by derobing, and thrust home low outside.

Cut over and one two (to deceive sixte and quarte).
Pass your bayonet over my point, I parry sixte; disengage, I parry quarte; deceive it, and thrust home in the sixte line.

Change to the Sixte Medium, and execute the feints from that line.

Engage in Quarte Medium.

Press and disengage (to deceive quarte).
Press my blade slightly, I resist this in the form of quarte; disengage, and thrust in sixte.

Press and derobe.
Press my blade slightly, I resist; derobe and thrust low.

Press and one two (to deceive quarte and sixte).	Press slightly, and on my resistance disengage, I parry sixte; deceive me by disengaging again, and thrust in the quarte line.
Beat and disengage (to deceive quarte).	Give a light "dry" beat on my blade, I resist in the form of quarte; disengage, and thrust in the sixte line.
Beat and derobe.	Give the dry beat, I resist it; derobe to the lower line and thrust.
Beat and one two (to deceive quarte and sixte).	Give the dry beat, I resist it; disengage, I parry sixte; disengage again, and thrust in the quarte line.
Change, beat, and derobe.	Change to sixte and instantly beat, I resist in sixte; derobe, and thrust low outside.
Change, beat, and disengage.	Change to sixte and beat, I resist in sixte; disengage and thrust in the quarte line.

Repeat the above movements from the sixte engagement.

As soon as the pupil is able to effect these compound attacks with precision, the master must cause him to practise them from the left guard.

I shall now proceed to apply the more simple of these feints, in combination with the returns, in the form of

Compound Ripostes, or Ripostes preceded by Feints.

Engage in Quarte Medium.

M.	*P.*
Thrust.	Parry quarte, disengage, and thrust in sixte line.
	On Guard.
Thrust.	Parry quarte, feint one two, thrust in the quarte line.
	On Guard.
Thrust.	Parry quarte, feint under and over, thrusting in quarte.
	On Guard.
Thrust.	Parry quarte, feint a straight thrust and derobe, thrusting in lower line.
	On Guard.

M.	*P.*
Disengage and thrust.	Parry sixte, disengage, and thrust in quarte line.
	On Guard.
Disengage and thrust.	Parry sixte, derobe, and thrust low outside.
	On Guard.
Disengage and thrust.	Parry sixte, feint one two, thrusting in sixte line.

COMBINATIONS.

Engage in Quarte Medium.

M.	*P.*
Thrust.	Parry quarte, derobe, and thrust low.
Parry septime, thrust high.	Parry quarte, disengage, and thrust.
Parry sixte.	

On Guard.

Reverse the lesson.

Thrust low.	Parry septime, thrust high.
Parry quarte, disengage, and thrust.	Parry sixte, derobe, and thrust.
Parry seconde.	

On Guard.

Reverse the lesson.

Disengage and throw.	Parry sixte, and thrust.
Parry sixte, disengage, and thrust.	Parry quarte, derobe, and thrust.
Parry septime.	

Guard.

Reverse the lesson.

M.	*P.*
Press.	On the pressure, disengage and thrust.
Parry septime, (arresting his movement), and thrust high.	Parry quarte, disengage and thrust.
Parry sixte.	

On Guard.

Reverse the lesson.

Press, disengage and thrust.	Parry sixte, disengage and thrust.
Parry quarte, thrust low.	Parry septime, thrust high.
Parry quarte.	

On Guard.

Reverse the lesson.

Froisse, and throw.	Parry quarte, thrust low.
Parry septime, thrust high.	Parry quarte, disengage and thrust.
Parry sixte.	

On Guard.

Reverse the lesson.

Beat (dry), disengage and thrust.	Parry sixte, disengage and thrust.
Parry quarte, one two, and thrust.	Parry quarte, feint under, thrust over.
Parry quarte.	

On Guard.

Reverse the lesson.

COMBINATIONS.

M.	*P.*
Change, froisse and throw.	Parry sixte, one two, and thrust.
Parry sixte, disengage and thrust.	Parry quarte, feint a thrust, and derobe.
Parry septime.	

On Guard.

Reverse the lesson.

Change, beat, disengage and thrust.	Parry quarte, thrust low.
Parry septime, thrust high.	Parry quarte, feint a thrust, and disengage.
Parry sixte.	

On Guard.

Reverse the lesson.

These combinations must be performed also from the left guard.

THE EDGES.

THE EDGES.

At the suggestion of the late Lord Strathnairn, I wrote in 1866 a short system of fence for the musket and sword-bayonet, which in 1867 I incorporated in my treatise, 'Swordsmanship and Bayonet-fencing.' In the following pages I shall adhere mainly to the rules therein laid down, adding certain matter which I deduce from my sabre lessons in 'Cold Steel.'

Circumstances occur but seldom when a direct attack may be safely made with the edge, and then only at the advanced hand or forearm when the opposing point is a little out of line; but the cut forms a powerful auxiliary in riposte when an overstrong parry on our part may have deflected our point somewhat away from the presence of our antagonist, as the Italians term it "fuor di presenza." Such deviation from the direct line is, in the case of a weapon pointed only, a grievous and very dangerous fault, as it renders a quick riposte impossible, while at the same time it leaves us open to a remise if we are engaged with an active man; but, with our present arm, a cut deftly substituted for the thrust in such a case makes our return hit a certainty.

I propose now six cuts, instead of four, as I

formerly advised: they are two diagonal downwards, two diagonal upwards, and two vertical cuts, one up and the other down, at the advanced hand and arm.

Cuts at the body are not, I think, advisable with a blade so short as ours, but they should be aimed at parts less likely to be protected by thick clothing.

The cuts, when delivered, should be finished with a drawing motion to make the edge bite; they are executed as follows:—

Cut 1 is given diagonally downwards, from right to left, at the left cheek, or neck, with the false edge.

Cut 2 is given diagonally downwards at the right cheek, or neck, from left to right, with the true edge.

Cut 3, or the "Coup de Jarnac," is given diagonally upwards, from right to left, at the sinews behind the advanced knee, with the false edge.

Cut 4 is given diagonally upwards, from left to right, at the advanced knee, with the true edge.

Cut 5 is directed vertically downwards at the advanced hand, or arm, with the true edge.

Cut 6 is directed vertically upwards at the advanced hand, or arm, with the false edge.

These two latter cuts, being vertical, may be made on either the inside or outside line.

PLATE XI.

THE BUTT-THRUST.

In this part of my system of bayonet-play I think it necessary to introduce a thrust with the *butt*, which I have derived from the "Ecole du Fantassin" of M. Gomard.

The Butt-thrust.

Allow the bayonet to drop to the rear over the left shoulder, pass forward the right foot, and drive the heelplate like a battering ram into the opponent's face.

The same French author also recommends a Back Butt-thrust (*coup de crosse en arriere*); this is not a thrust of fencing, but is intended to be used in a *melée*, when attacked from behind so suddenly and so closely that there is no possibility of bringing the rifle "about" in order to employ the point. Without moving the feet, turn the body and head to the rear, and with the full swing of the arms force the heelplate into the face of the assailant.

SUPPLEMENTARY PARRIES.

The Parry of Prime against Cut 1.

CUT 1, when returned over the rifle after having parried quarte, is very difficult to stop; it must be parried with *Prime*, a movement which corresponds to the "High Prime" of the sabre (*vide* 'Cold Steel'). Drop the point and raise the butt, until the weapon is nearly vertical, but with the point inclined a little forward, and turn the stock to the left front, allowing the rifle to revolve in the left hand; the right hand, which holds the small, must now be as high as the top of the head, so that you can look at the enemy underneath the wrist; the left, or advanced hand, must be slided nearly to the muzzle; and the cut must be received on the centre, between the hands.

The Parry of High Septime against Cut 2.

Cut 2, when returned over the rifle after having parried sixte, is even more difficult to stop than the corresponding cut on the other side, being, I think, more rapid, and certainly much more powerful; it must be parried with *High Septime*. Drop the point and raise the butt until the weapon is nearly vertical, but

PLATE XII.

THE PARRY OF PRIME.

PLATE XIII.

THE PARRY OF HIGH SEPTIME.

with the point a little advanced, and turn the stock to the right front; the right hand, holding the small, must be as high as the top of the head, and the left hand must be slided nearly to the muzzle, and Cut 2 must be received on the centre.

THE PARRY OF UNDER-SIXTE AGAINST CUT 3.

Cut 3, which is directed at the outside of the advanced knee after having parried rather wide in septime, must be parried with the *Under Sixte.* Raise the point and drop the butt to the left front, shift the fingers of the right hand (as suggested by Selmnitz) in such a manner that the small shall be momentarily held between the thumb and the centre joint of the forefinger, and receive Cut 3 on the butt, and the instant the parry is effected the proper grip must be resumed; it will be found that as the riposte is being given the fingers of the right hand will readily resume their normal position, just as is the case after the parry of "High Octave" in Sabre Play (*vide* 'Cold Steel').

This parry of *under-sixte* is also extremely useful, as shown by M. le Capitaine Chatin, a French officer, in his excellent little work 'L'Escrime à la Baïonnette,' published in 1855, for *parrying thrusts at the lower line*, especially the outer, the attacking point being dashed aside by a sweep of the butt from right to left.

The Parry of Under-quarte against Cut 4.

Cut 4 is parried with the butt in under-quarte. Raise the point and drop the butt to right front, shifting the grip of the right hand as before, and receive on the butt.

I have named these two parries *under-quarte* and *under-sixte*, to distinguish them from low-quarte and low-sixte, which would relate to the *forte* of the weapon.

To Defend the Advanced Hand from Cut 5.

The only secure method of meeting this vertical downward cut at the advanced hand is by slipping it back and delivering a time-thrust in the form of a throw.

To Defend the Advanced Hand from Cut 6.

For this there are two defences; first, by the parry of *horizontal quarte*, bring the rifle horizontally across the body, with the stock downwards, and receive Cut 6 on the centre; second, by shifting the hand and delivering the time-throw.

PLATE XIV.

THE PARRY OF UNDER-SIXTE.

PLATE XV.

THE PARRY OF UNDER-QUARTE.

PLATE XVI.

THE PARRY OF HORIZONTAL QUARTE.

PLATE XVII.

THE PARRY OF HORIZONTAL PRIME.

The parries of centre-sixte and centre-quarte are sometimes useful in a "*phrase d'armes;*" they are formed with the point raised, the parry being effected with the centre, or the part of the rifle between the two hands.

The Parry of Horizontal Prime against the Butt-thrust.

Bring the rifle horizontally across the body, the bayonet pointing to the left; turn the stock upwards, and, with the centre, force up the attacking butt so as to be clear of the head.

This thrust may on occasion be parried with quarte or sixte.

These cuts and parries should be practised on the left guard.

COMBINATIONS ON THE FOREGOING LESSONS.

Engage in Quarte Medium.

M.	*P.*
1. Thrust.	Parry quarte, cut 1 over the rifle.
Parry prime, thrust.	Parry seconde, cut 4.
Parry under-quarte.	
	On Guard.
Reverse the lesson.	
2. Thrust.	Parry quarte, cut 1 over the rifle.
Parry prime, thrust prime.	Parry sixte or centre-sixte, cut 2.
Parry quarte.	
	On Guard.
Reverse the lesson.	
3. Disengage and thrust.	Parry sixte, cut 2 over the rifle.
Parry high septime, thrust low.	Parry under-sixte, thrust butt.
Avoid by slipping.	
	On Guard.
Reverse the lesson.	

M.	*P.*
4. Derobe and thrust low.	Parry septime, cut 3.
Parry under-sixte, cut 2.	Parry high septime, thrust low (by sinking down to it).
Parry under sixte.	
	On Guard.
Reverse the lesson.	
5. Cut over and derobe.	Parry seconde, cut 4.
Parry under-quarte, cut 1.	Parry prime, thrust low (by sinking down).
Parry under-quarte.	
	On Guard.
Reverse the lesson.	

MOVEMENTS WITH ADVANCED HAND.

M.	*P.*
Cut 5.	Slip the hand back, and deliver the throw as a time hit.
Cut 6.	Slip the hand, and time as above.
Cut 6.	Parry horizontal quarte, and cut 2 over the rifle.
Cut 6.	Parry horizontal quarte, and thrust butt.

A SYSTEM OF BUTT-FENCING.

BUTT-FENCING.

SEVERAL Continental writers have advocated, from time to time, certain blows with the butt to be used in cases of emergency, but I have not as yet found among their works anything approaching to a system of attack and defence with that part of the weapon.

In 1882, however, I published in my 'Bayonet-fencing and Sword-practice,' a rudimentary arrangement of "strokes" and "stops;" this I shall now enlarge upon, applying to the "stops," or rather *parries*, the customary terms of fence to which I have systematically adhered, both in the earlier portion of this book and also in its predecessor, 'Cold Steel.'

There must arise, whether in a fight with sharps, or in a friendly contest in the fencing-room, occasions on which the combatants find themselves so close together that neither of them can, with anything like safety, attempt either to withdraw his person or disentangle his weapon. This I have often seen in a bout of play, and, indeed, more than once in public, when the men were so utterly nonplussed that they were obliged to separate by mutual consent—an arrangement easy enough in the mimic fight of the *salle d'armes*, but not quite so feasible in a life-and-death struggle in the field; and it is in such-like cases that the system which I designate "Butt-fencing" will be found most effective; indeed, a bold man who understands it thoroughly will be rather inclined to court a close, feeling that he has within his grasp a method of "*Corps à corps*" fighting which is superior to any method of "Shortening arms" ever yet invented.

The Attacks.

The attacks in butt-fencing consist of certain "strokes," which must be given with the sharp projecting "toe" only. A blow with this is very conclusive, and its force is felt even when it falls on a stout fencing-helmet; any injury is, however, obviated entirely by the use of the very simple padded butts which were devised according to my suggestions some years ago, and have been in use at the London Fencing Club ever since. If the stroke is given with any part other than the sharp "toe," it can do no harm beyond irritating the recipient, and making him perhaps a little more dangerous.

In addition to the strokes, we have the thrusts which I have already described, inflicted with the heel-plate, these are similar to the "coups de crosse" recommended by Chapitre, who emphasises the fact of their being thrusts by connecting with them the command "Pointez."

These attacks must be made according as openings are discovered, and at parts of the person only on which blows with an obtuse weapon will tell seriously, such as the face and head, the "horseshoe," the points of the lower ribs, and behind on the kidneys; they must all be given direct, as I think it will be found impossible to combine feints with them.

Guard.

I shall suppose the rifles to be crossed at their centres in the quarte position, this being the one in which the combatants are most likely to find themselves on coming to close quarters, and which, therefore, we must consider to be our "guard."

We must recollect, further, that, when once we have made up our minds to fight with the butt, we must keep close in and prevent our man from getting away, lest he should find the opportunity of "shortening arms" and treating us to his point.

Stroke 1.

Rapidly sink the point, raise the butt, and deliver the stroke with the "toe" above the opponent's rifle, at his left cheek or temple.

Stroke 2.

Raise the point until the rifle is very nearly vertical, and drive the "toe" either into his "horseshoe" (the pit of the stomach), or the points of his lower ribs.

Stroke 3.

Pass forward the right foot, and deliver the toe behind the left ear; this is useful when, from the position of his rifle and left arm, you are not likely to succeed with stroke 1 or stroke 2.

Stroke 4.

Pass forward the right foot and deliver the stroke just below the ribs on the left rear.

The Thrust.

This movement is the same as the thrust previously described, save that, the combatants being close together, the step forward is unnecessary.

THE PARRIES.

Against Stroke 1.

Raise the butt, throwing the stock upwards, into the form of prime, and receive stroke 1 on the centre.

PLATE XVIII.

BUTT-FENCING.—THE GUARD.

PLATE XIX.

BUTT-FENCING.—STROKE I.

PLATE XX.

BUTT-FENCING.—STROKE 2.

PLATE XXI

BUTT-FENCING.—STROKE 3.

PLATE XXII.

BUTT-FENCING.—STROKE 4.

PLATE XXIII.

BUTT-FENCING.—POSITION IN PARRYING STROKES 3 AND 4, WITH SIXTE AND CENTRE-SIXTE.

Against Stroke 2.

Bring the rifle to the position of horizontal quarte, and receive stroke 2 on the centre.

Against Stroke 3.

Raise the rifle to a vertical position, in the form of sixte, the left hand to be as high as, and close to, the left shoulder, and receive stroke 3 on the forte.

Against Stroke 4.

Lower the butt, and bring the rifle to a vertical position, in the form of sixte, as above, and receive stroke 4 with centre-sixte between the hands.

Against the Thrust.

Bring the rifle to the position of horizontal prime, and force the opponent's butt upwards with the centre. The thrust may on occasion be parried with the forte in quarte or in sixte.

Stroke 2 may be used as a feint, in order to draw the horizontal quarte parry, and a drawing cut 2 be made at the right cheek.

COMBINATIONS OF STROKES, RIPOSTES AND CONTRE-RIPOSTES.

M.	*P.*
Stroke 1.	Parry prime, stroke 2.
Horizontal quarte, stroke 1.	Parry prime.
	On Guard.
Reverse the lesson.	
Stroke 2.	Parry horizontal quarte, stroke 1.
Parry prime, stroke 2.	Parry horizontal quarte.
	On Guard.
Reverse the lesson.	
Stroke 3.	Parry sixte, stroke 2.
Parry horizontal quarte and stroke 1.	Parry prime.
	On Guard.
Reverse the lesson.	
Stroke 4.	Parry centre sixte, stroke 1.
Parry prime, stroke 2.	Parry horizontal quarte.
	On Guard.
Reverse the lesson.	

M.	*P.*
Thrust.	Parry horizontal prime, stroke 2.
Parry horizontal quarte, stroke 1.	Parry prime.

On Guard.

Reverse the lesson.

COMBINATIONS FOR RIGHT GUARD OPPOSED TO LEFT GUARD.

I THINK it advisable now to record a few combinations intended to facilitate a combat with a left-handed man, in which *M.* will take the right guard and *P.* the left guard. When the lesson is reversed, *P.* will of course stand on the right guard and *M.* on the left.

M., Right Guard.	*P.*, Left Guard.
Thrust outside high.	Parry sixte, cut at left cheek.
Parry prime, cut outside leg.	Parry under sixte, cut right cheek.
Parry quarte.	

On Guard.

Reverse the lesson.

Thrust inside high.	Parry quarte, cut at right temple.
Parry horizontal prime, butt stroke at left ear.	Parry quarte, stroke 2 at ribs.
Parry horizontal quarte.	

On Guard.

Reverse the lesson.

Thrust low.   Parry septime, thrust low.
Parry under-sixte, cut at   Parry horizontal prime,
  head.   thrust prime outside high.
Parry sixte.

On Guard.

Reverse the lesson.

Thrust low.   Parry septime, thrust high.
Parry quarte, cut left   Parry high septime, pass,
  cheek.   and give the butt at the
            right cheek.

Parry quarte.

THE ASSAULT.

THE ASSAULT.

THE necessary personal equipment for bayonet-fencing is similar to that used in sabre play, with the addition of a stout fencing gauntlet for the left hand.

When leg pads are worn, hits should count as good ones on whatever part they may strike, but when the leg pads are dispensed with, no hit must be allowed at or below the knee, in order to obviate the danger of inflicting serious injury.

A *time hit* should only be counted good where it saves the giver from being touched at all; when both touch, and the intended time thrust is only a matter of half a second or so in advance of the other, it should not be counted, as both men would have been killed, but the two should be treated as exchanged hits or "coups fourrés." A *time hit* at the advanced leg with any weapon is not to be recommended, and, indeed, should not be allowed at all; it would never be attempted with sharps, being far too dangerous.

When a hit is received, the player who receives it should *acknowledge* by dropping his point to the ground, quitting the hold with, and extending the left hand, palm uppermost; he who has given the hit should immediately recover to guard.

In loose play, the combatants must be especially careful to preserve due elasticity of joint and limb, by avoiding any pressure or contact of the hands or arms with the body, except, of course, in the case of the "Resting Guard."

In making the Assault, I am inclined to take the "Guard" with the point a little more horizontal than when performing the set lessons; but, excepting when engaged against the sabre, the point must never be held in the low lines, a position which would attract a downward beat—and that, if successful, would most likely crush the barrel, and so ruin the rifle for shooting purposes, the preservation of which should be one of our first cares.

When the combatants engage with "opposition," that is, with the weapons crossed and covering either line, they should avoid any *accidental or involuntary pressure* upon the opposing rifle; pressure of this kind is exceedingly dangerous, as it lays them open to an attack by either "disengagement" or "cut over." Pressure, however, with the weapon under thorough control, may be resorted to as before described, both to force an opening, and as a feint to draw either responding pressure or a disengagement. Men engaged with this opposition should be ready, in case of disengagement, either to parry in the opposite line, or, what is still more baffling to the enemy, to arrest his movement by a parry in the corresponding low line—as, for instance, I engage in quarte with opposition, you disengage, and I, instead of allowing you to complete your attack and parrying it with sixte, stop your movement half way by the parry of septime, and if you "derobe" on this and thrust high, I come up to quarte again, and so keep you captive on the inner lines, whether you will or no.

The Attack should always be commenced with *point*, excepting at the advanced hand, and this is not to be recommended unless the opponent's point is a little off the line; but in riposte, the edge is, as has been shown, very useful indeed, especially where the point has been allowed to deviate from the line, a breach of fencing rule which the Bayonet Exercise of 1889, practically speaking, enforces.

Engage always out of distance, and advance with little short steps, keeping the point always threatening the enemy; and if you find that he is given to retiring, pursue him steadily, securing always the ground he has lost in his retreat; and when there may be broken ground or other obstacle somewhere in rear of him, force him upon it by means of the traverse (see 'Cold Steel,' p. 7). An opponent who is given to retiring much, will probably have recourse a good deal to the "throw," in which be ready with a strong parry, especially in the outer lines, as in them his recovery of the control of his weapon is more difficult; and advance upon him promptly before he can come to Guard. Where the antagonist seems inclined to come within measure, it is probable that he has the design to "Shorten arms" upon you, and therefore it may be wise to be beforehand with him by enclosing rapidly before he can draw his weapon sufficiently back, and treating him with the butt; if he does not understand "Butt-fencing," you can do what you will with him, and if he does understand it, you are on equal terms again.

If the enemy is a bold man and given to attacking, it is better to await him in the defensive position, without, if possible, giving ground, and trusting mainly to your parry and riposte, this latter being the most certain hit in fencing with any arm. In point play it is well to break off the "*phrase d'armes*" after three or four thrusts have been exchanged, either by enclosing and coming to butt-fencing, or by springing back to guard out of reach, because, the weapon being a heavy one, the play after a rally of any considerable duration is sure to become disorganised, and the parries and ripostes will lose both their velocity and their precision.

In recovery after making an attack, come back to guard always with "opposition," that is to say, covering one line completely, after which resume whatever guard suits you best.

The time in which it is best to attack, is the time when you perceive that the enemy is meditating and preparing an attack upon you; he will be thinking of nothing else, and will therefore be off his guard.

BAYONET AGAINST SABRE.

BAYONET AGAINST SABRE.

THE decrease in the length of our bayonet must alter very considerably the relations between these two arms. Formerly, owing to the reach of our weapon, we were able to keep the swordsman at a great distance, while the momentum of our thrust was such as to oblige a parry on his part so strong as in most cases to prevent his giving his riposte with the required celerity. With the new arm, however, we are robbed of our main advantage, namely, reach, but we have a set-off for it in our two edges.

We are so near to the swordsman that he may, without much risk, deliver delicate little cuts with either of his edges at our advanced hand, and of this we should be extremely careful. Should he attempt them—and if he knows his business he most assuredly will do so—we must shift the hand and treat him to time thrusts, as an attempt at a parry, either in Horizontal Prime or Horizontal Quarte, would be too risky, as it would give him an opportunity of "commanding" our weapon on the pass at its centre; it is true that we might baffle his attempt to command by meeting him with either butt or edge, but I think the slip and time thrust are preferable.

He may, again, only feint a cut at the advanced hand, in order to draw our time thrust, which it is seen must be a "throw," and therefore our left hand must be in perfect readiness to resume instant and complete control of our rifle; and never, in any case, must we allow ourselves to fall into the trap which the military authorities have set for us by their absurd order to withdraw the advanced hand entirely and "grasp the thigh" with it.

We must hold our point rather low, and a little away from the exact line of direction, but still not entirely deviated from the presence of the opponent, and we should keep our weapon slightly in motion, in order to promote elasticity, which will *not* be effected by holding the right hand fixed to the hip; otherwise he will attempt, and very likely succeed, in engaging and controlling our weapon with his sword in tierce or seconde, and that done will inevitably pass forward and try to command our rifle at its centre, and therefore, if we allow him to move forward, we must meet him by passing forward also, and delivering a crushing No. 1 stroke in his face with the butt. It is better, however, when he attempts to engage and cross our bayonet, to disengage and give him the point.

We ought to have the advantage of him, for we have three modes of attack, namely, point, edge, and butt, where he has only the edge and point; but it is incumbent upon us to be very well skilled in the practice of all three—and this the military authorities and their imitators, the Council of the Royal Military Tournament, have hitherto denied to us.

AGAINST THE LONG BAYONET.

AGAINST THE LONG BAYONET.

A MAN armed with a weapon of the old-fashioned length—some six feet—has, it must be allowed, an advantage over us in reach, but we, with our shorter weapon, have that of lightness.

The opponent will naturally play to keep us at a distance, knowing that his foot or so of additional cold steel is then of most use to him; he will probably also have recourse to extended "throws." We, with our shorter weapon, must trust at first entirely to our facility in parrying; we must advance by degrees within distance, keeping him captive,* by the use of opposition in Quarte, supported by Septime, constantly on the inside, which is the easiest for us to defend; and we must take special care to prevent an attack on our advanced hand, while we must deliver such an attack upon him with our edge at the first opportunity. Or we may feint a cut at his hand, in order to draw the time thrust, which we must parry, and return with point, still creeping in upon him and getting well within distance; having attained which, we shall find that an attack by "shortening arms" will be

* See Glossary.

much easier for us with our short blade than for him with his long one; and, if this does not appear feasible, we can enclose still further, and commence action with the butt. Again, in retiring from the "corps à corps" position, it being supposed that our butt-fight has resulted in a drawn game, we shall be able to resume point play sooner than he will. In fact, excepting at the very first commencement of the encounter, when his long reach tells in his favour, a bold, active, determined man, armed with the shorter weapon, will have the advantage; but to secure it he will need much more thorough instruction in the art of bayonet-fencing than that provided in the Bayonet Exercise of 1889.

GLOSSARY.

A GLOSSARY OF ENGLISH, FRENCH, AND ITALIAN TECHNICAL TERMS OF FENCE.

(Fr.) French; (It.) Italian; (Obs.) Obsolete.

S'ABANDONNER (Fr.). To act in manner not conformable to the rules of Fencing or the directions of the master.

ABORDER (Fr.). To advance towards the adversary for the purpose of assuming the offensive.

ABSENCE (Fr.). The momentary quitting the adversary's blade in order to deprive him of the advantage of touch.

ACADEMICAL (Style). Is the style possessed by a fencer who strictly adheres, in all his movements, to those of the lessons he has received from a first-rate master.

ADVANCE, TO. To approach your antagonist, when on guard, with little short steps.

ADVERSAIRE (Fr.). Opponent.

AFFONDO (It.). See Lunge.

ALLER À L'EPÉE (Fr.). To follow all the movements of the opponent's sword, whether good or bad.

ALLONGEMENT (Fr.). Extension.

À MOI (Fr.). An exclamation used by loyal fencers to acknowledge a hit when received.

ANNONCER (Fr.). To acknowledge a hit by exclaiming "À moi," "Touché," &c.

APPÂT (Fr.). A great opening shown for the purpose of attracting a particular attack.

APPEL (Fr.). A smart stamp on the ground made with the advanced foot, either with a view of frightening the opponent, or of ascertaining that one is oneself well placed on guard.

APPUNTATA (It.). (See Remise.)

ARRESTO, COLPO DI (It.). (See Coup d'Arrêt.)

ASSAILLANT (Fr.). The party who takes the initiative in coming to the attack.

ASSAULT.
ASSAUT (Fr.).
ASSALTO (It.).
{ The exercise with blunt weapons, representing in every respect a combat with sharps, in which we execute at will all the manœuvres of the fencing lessons.

ASSAULT OF ARMS.
ASSAUT D'ARMES (Fr.).
} An exhibition of fencing with various weapons.

ATTACK, SIMPLE. An attack made direct, without any previous movement to cause an opening.

ATTACK, COMPOUND. An attack preceded by feints or other movements made to cause an opening where there is none.

ATTACK, SINGLE AND DOUBLE. (See Appel.) The double attack consists of two consecutive beats on the ground, the first being given with the heel, and the second with the fore part of the foot.

AVOIR DES JAMBES (Fr.). To be well set on one's legs.

AVOIR DE LA MAIN (Fr.). To possess the faculty of guiding the sword delicately with the action of the fingers instead of using the coarser movements of the wrist and arm.

AVOIR DE LA TÊTE (Fr.). Is to use judgment and discrimination in divining the intentions of the opponent, and in setting traps to frustrate them.

AVOIR UNE PARADE DANS LA MAIN (Fr.). Is to have some pet parry which one instinctively forms in preference to others; this is a fault which is easily worked upon by an opponent who fences with his head. It is a fault, too, which is very much caused by those teachers who seek to simplify the art by cutting down the number, and therefore the variety, of the defensive movements.

BACKSWORD (Obs.). A sword with a broad back, edge, and short false edge, so called in contradistinction, to the "shearing" sword, which had both edges sharp from hilt to point; it was the favourite arm of the "gladiators" of the eighteenth century.

BASKET. (See Bucket.) Originally this protection for the hand was made of wicker work, not only in England, but also, according to Diderot and Chatelain, in France, down to the early part of this century.

BASKET-HILT. A close sword-hilt, like that of the Highland broadsword. The term "half-basket," used to be applied to a hilt somewhat resembling that of the modern sabre.

BATTEMENT (Fr.). } (See Beat.)
BATTUTA (It.).

BAYONET-FENCING (Fr.). The art of attack and defence with the rifle and fixed bayonet, in which everything—point, edge, and butt—are brought into play.

BEAT. A light, lateral blow given to the opponent's weapon in order to force an opening.

BERSAGLIO (It.). An opening.

BINDING. A method of forcing an opening, sometimes called "Flançonnade," where the opponent holds his sword horizontally and his arm straight, formed by opposing his foible in "quarte" with your forte, circling your blade round his, but without quitting it, and pressing his point to your right, your own sword assuming the position of "seconde" or "octave." When, however, in attempting this bind, you find your forte opposed to his forte instead of his foible, recourse must be had to the "croise," by passing your hilt over his blade, the two swords being parallel to each other, and striking him on the reverse side of his weapon in the lower line.

BLINDFOLD LESSONS. Lessons of defence in which the eyes of the pupil are shut, or even bandaged, in order to make him work by touch only (*vide* 'Cold Steel,' p. 237).

BONDIR (Fr.). To advance or retire abruptly, by jumping either to the front or the rear from both feet at once.

BOTTE (Fr., obs.). A completed thrust.

BOTTA DRITTA (It.). A straight thrust without any change of line.

BOUT. An encounter in loose play.

BOUTON (Fr.). (See Button.)

BRAS RACCOURCI (Fr.). The act of drawing back the sword arm in order to avoid the enemy's parry, or to make a more violent thrust. A man who has constant recourse to this dangerous trick ought not to be allowed to fence.

BREAK GROUND OR MEASURE. To retire precipitately on being attacked.

BRETTEUR (Fr.). A bully. The term is sometimes applied to one who fences in a rough, coarse style.

BROADSWORD. A sword used both for cutting and thrusting.

BROCCHIERO (It.). (See Buckler.)

BRUSH. (See Frolé.)

BUCKET. The bowl-shaped shell of hide used to protect the hand when playing single-stick.

BUCKLER. A small shield, sometimes round in form and sometimes square, which was carried in the left *hand*, not on the arm, and was used in old times, in conjunction with the broadsword, for the purpose of parrying.

BUTTON. The little round plate of metal at the point of a foil.

CAMBIARE (It.). (See Change.)

CAPOT, FAIRE (Fr.).
CAPOTTO, DAR (It.).
} To beat an opponent so thoroughly that he never touches one at all; to make him, in fact, score a "duck's egg."

CAPTIF (Fr.).
CAPTIVER (Fr.).
CAPTIVE.
} To keep your opponent, against his will, on one side of your weapon only.

CAVEATING (Obs.). Disengaging.

CAVAZIONE (It.). Disengagement.

CAVER (Fr.). This movement is the direct contrary to "opposition." It consists of carrying the hand out of the line during the attack in such a manner as to cause the blade to form an obtuse angle with the sword arm; it is extremely dangerous, as it leaves the very opening which the "opposition" completely closes.

CEDER L'EPÉE (Fr.). To avoid anything in the shape of resistance or response to "pressure" from the opposing blade, and to "derobe" directly such pressure is felt.

CENTRE (Bayonet-fencing). That part of the rifle which lies between the balance and the small of the butt.

CENTRE OF PERCUSSION. Is that part of a sabre blade which should strike the object at which the cut is directed; it is situated near the point, about three-quarters of the length of the blade from the hilt. A cut given with any part of the blade above or below this point loses its effect from defective leverage.

CHANGE.
CHANGER (Fr.).
} To alter the engagement from "quarte" to "sixte," or *vice versâ*, by dipping underneath the opposing blade, and joining it again on the other side.

CHASSE-COQUIN (Fr.). A slang term for a very stiff foil, reserved for use against rough, brutal fencers, or such as are in the habit of denying hits.

CHASSER LES MOUCHES (Fr.). Is to lose one's head when feints are made, and to be betrayed into making violent and disorganised movements of the sword hand, as if trying to frighten away flies.

CIRCLES. Parries formed by circling the blade under that of the opponent on his disengaging, and chasing it back into its previous line, instead of defending with a simple parry.

COMBINATIONS. Set lessons consisting of various series of attacks, parries and ripostes, &c., used for the purpose of advancing the pupil towards loose play.

COMMAND, TO. To dominate or control either the person or the weapon of the opponent with either blade or hand. (*Vide* 'Cold Steel,' p. 89.)

COMPOUND ATTACKS. (See Attacks.)

COMPOUND PARRIES. A series of defensive movements which follow all the movements of a compound attack until the "parade" is completed effectually.

CONTRACTION. In foil or sword play this term is applied to any parry which crosses or arrests the movement of the attacking blade instead of following its movements.

CONTRES (Fr.).
CONTRI (It.).
COUNTERS.
} Circular parries.

CONTRE-DÉGAGEMENT (Fr.).
CONTRO-CAVAZIONE (It.).
COUNTER-DISENGAGEMENT.
} A second disengagement to deceive the "contre," or circular parry.

CORPS À CORPS (Fr.). The position in which the combatants are when they have approached so close that it is possible for them to seize hold of each other.

COUCHER, SE (Fr.). To avoid a thrust by bending the body forward.

COULÉ (Fr.). A direct thrust effected by means of a prolonged pressure, the blade gliding down that of the opponent until the point is level and the arm straight.

COUNTER-TIME. A simulated attack made in order to draw a time hit, which we parry and then complete our attack.

COUNTER-HIT. A hit given instead of parrying when the opponent attacks. It is a very great fault.

COUNTER-CAVEATING (Obs.). An old term for any circular parry formed upon the adversary's disengagement.

COUP (Fr.). The series of movements which the weapon makes in order to arrive at the opponent's body.

COUP DE BOUTON (Fr.). A touch with a foil.

COUP D'EPÉE (Fr.). A sword thrust.

COUP DE SABRE (Fr.). A sabre cut.

COUP DE FIGURE (Fr.). A cut at the face.

COUP DE BANDEROLE (Fr.). A cut at the shoulder and breast.

COUP DE FLANC (Fr.). A cut at the right side.

COUP DE MANCHETTE (Fr.). A cut at the wrist.

COUP DE JARNAC (Fr.). A cut at the leg. (See Jarnac.)

COUP DE TÊTE (Fr.). A cut at the head.

COUP DE VENTRE (Fr.). A cut at the left side.

COUP COMPOSÉ (Fr.). Compound attack. (See Attack.)

COUP D'ARRÊT (Fr.). The stop thrust, which is made in order to stop the opponent when he attacks with complicated movements, &c.

COUP DROIT (Fr.). A direct attack made without any change of line.

COUPS FOURRÉS (Fr.). Interchanged hits, when both attack at the same moment.

COUP DE TEMPS (Fr.). A time hit, which is effected just as the opponent is meditating an attack, or when he comes forward with movements either too wide or too slow.

COUP SIMPLE (Fr.). A plain attack made with or without a disengagement, but without any movement to effect an opening.

COUP PASSÉ (Fr.). An attack which misses its mark altogether.

COUPER (Fr.). To "Cut over." To make an attack by passing the blade over the opponent's point into the opposite line.

COURT SWORD. The light, triangular, pointed weapon employed by the French in their affairs of honour. It, or a form of it, came into fashion about the time of Charles II. It is mentioned by Marcelli, of Rome, 1686, under the name of "la spada corta" (Fr., l'epée courte), in contradistinction to "la spada," the long rapier, which it very soon supplanted in most countries in Europe.

COUVERT (Fr.). } Is to be so placed on guard that you cannot be
COVERED. } touched by a straight thrust.

CROISÉ (Fr.). (See Binding.)

CROISER, SE (Fr.). To cross the right foot over the line of the left, either when on guard or on the lunge; a faulty position which tends to loss of balance.

COWARD'S GUARD (Obs.). This was a term of contempt used by the backswordsmen of the Eighteenth Century, for the old-fashioned "hanging-guard" which was much more adapted to defence than to attack.

CUDGELLING (Obs.). The name of an old-fashioned game nearly resembling modern singlestick.

CUT OVER. (See Couper.)

DECEIVE, TO. Is, after having produced on the part of the opponent one or more movements of defence, to avoid them just as they are on the point of touching your blade.

DÉCOLLER, SE (Fr.). Is, after having parried, to detach one's blade at once from that of the opponent, in order to effect a riposte.

DECOUVERT (Fr.). Uncovered; holding the weapon in such a manner that one can be hit with a straight thrust.

DEDANS (Fr.). Within; it is the space on the left side of the sword as we stand on guard—the reverse, of course, in the case of a left-handed man.

DEGAGEMENT (Fr.). An attack on the opposite, made by dipping the point under the opponent's blade.

DEHORS (Fr.). The space on the right of the sword when engaged.

DÉROBER (Fr.). To thrust in the low line, after making a feint, beat, or pressure, by dropping the point as the opposing blade responds.

DÉSARMER (Fr.). To disarm; to cause the opponent's weapon to fall from his hand.

DESSOUS (Fr.). In the lower lines.

DESSUS (Fr.). In the upper lines.

DETENTE (Fr.). The action of the muscles which, like a spring, starts the development of the lunge.

DÉVELOPPEMENT (Fr.). (See Lunge.)

DISENGAGE. (See Degagement.)

DISORDINATA (It.) Making, in sabre play, more than two feints in the same attack.

DISTANCE. (See Measure.)

DOIGTÉ (Fr.). The delicate management of the sword by the action of the fingers in attacking or parrying.

DONNER LE FER (Fr.). To engage frankly with the sword in the correct position, so that the opponent can join it without inconvenience.

DOUBLER (Fr.). To deceive a circular parry by a second disengagement.

DROITIER (Fr.). A right-handed fencer.

S'ÉBRANLER (Fr.). To lose one's head.

ÉCARTER (Fr.). To move either point or body out of the direct line.

S'EFFACER (Fr.). To throw back the left shoulder in such a manner that the breast cannot be fairly touched.

ENGAGEMENT. The act of joining blades with the opponent, foible crossing foible; this is the signal that both combatants are ready.

GLOSSARY.

Épée (Fr.). Sword; the triangular, pointed weapon used in the duel.

Épée de Salle (Fr.). A weapon similar to the sword, but having a button at the point; it is used in fencing rooms for the practice of the duelling play.

Escrime (Fr.). The art of attack and defence with any kind of weapon held in the hand.

Escrimeur (Fr.). A swordsman complete in every detail.

Espadon (Fr., obs.). A sabre.

Eviter (Fr.). To dodge a hit, by ducking, twisting the body, &c.

Exchanged Hits. (See Coups fourrés.)

Extension. An attack made by straightening the sword arm and bracing the left knee, without lunging.

Faire des Armes (Fr.). To fence.

False Attack. A sham attack made with a half lunge, or with the extension only, in order to induce the enemy to show his favourite parries.

False Guard. The guard in tierce with the great stick (*vide* 'Cold Steel,' p. 151).

False Edge. The sharp part of the back of a sabre (*vide* 'Cold Steel,' p. 3).

Falso Dritto (It., obs.). In the old rapier practice this was an oblique ascending cut from right to left, given with the false edge.

Falso Manco (It., obs.). An oblique ascending cut in rapier play, from left to right, given with the false edge.

Fausse Attaque (Fr.). (See False attack.)

Feeling. To feel the opponent's blade is to keep a touch on it so delicate and so entirely free from force or pressure that one is sensible to its slightest movement. A complete set of lessons for the cultivation of this will be found in the "Blindfold Lessons" in the Appendix to 'Cold Steel.'

Feints. Simulated attacks made at various points in order to draw the parry, while the real attack is directed at the opening left by it.

Fendre, Se (Fr.). To lunge.

Fencing. (See Escrime.)

Fendente (It.). A cleaving, or vertical downward cut.

Ferrailleur (Fr.). A coarse, brutal, ignorant fencer

Fleuret (Fr.). The foil; the weapon of the fencing-room with which the art of using the sword (*epée*) is studied.

Fianconnata (It.). (See Binding.)

Figure of Eight. A double circle performed with the sabre, useful for keeping off an opponent in the dark (*vide* 'Cold Steel,' p. 29).

Filo di Spada (It.). The Italians give this name to all the "binds," of which they practise many more than we do, excepting that of "flançonnade," which is described in this work under the head of Binding.

Finta (It.). (See Feint.)

First Position. The position we assume previous to coming on guard.

Flançonnade. (See Binding.)

Flying Point. A movement consisting of a parry followed instantly by a "cut over;" the term is not much used at the present day.

Foible. The half of the sword, between the centre and the point, with which all cuts are effected.

Forconare (It.). To draw the hand back and attempt to gain a hit by stabbing as if with a poniard.

Forte. The half of the blade, between the hilt and centre, with which all parries are formed. The part of the rifle between the muzzle and the "balance."

Foul Blow. An unfair hit given when the opponent is not ready (*vide* 'Cold Steel,' p. 234).

Frase (It.). (See Phrase d'armes.)

Froissement (Fr.). A beat made by striking the foible of the opponent's sword, and forcing one's blade down it; it is much more powerful than the simple beat.

Frolé (Fr.) is the term applied to a thrust which does not fix fairly on the body, but slips along; it is not reckoned a good hit.

Fuor di presenza (It.). Out of line.

GAME OF THE SWORD. The art of fencing with a buttoned sword, as in a duel (*vide* 'Cold Steel,' p. 127).

GAUCHER (Fr.). A left-handed fencer.

GLISSÉ DE L'ARME (Fr.) is the term used by French writers on Bayonet-fencing to describe that "throw point" in delivering which the rifle is made to glide along the open palm of the left hand.

GLIZADE. An attack on the blade with a sliding motion, as in the "Coulé" or the "Froissement."

GREAT STICK. A stick about five feet in length, which is held at the end with both hands (*vide* 'Cold Steel,' p. 145).

GUARD.
GARDE (Fr.).   That position of person and weapon which is the most ready for both attack and defence.
GUARDIA (It.).

GUARD, TO. To protect with a parry the part of the person attacked. We *guard* the part, but we *parry* the blow.

GUIDER, SE (Fr.). To regulate one's movements according to those of one's opponent.

HALF CIRCLE. (See Septime.)

HELMET. The strong mask which protects the whole of the head; used in sabre play, bayonet fencing, and such-like heavy work.

HIGH LINES. The lines on both sides of the blade, above the hand.

IMBROCCATA (It., obs.). In the days of the rapier this term was applied to thrusts made above the opponent's blade with the hand in pronation, as in the modern thrust in Tierce.

INCONTRO (It.) An exchanged hit.

IN-FIGHTING.
IN-PLAY.   This term properly appertains to the art of boxing, but in Bayonet-fencing it is to be applied to the act of closing the measure in order to get within the opponent's guard, so as to make use of the butt or edge.

INQUARTATA (It.). (See Volte.)

INCITO (It.). An opening shown to induce the opponent to attack.

JET DE L'ARME (Fr.) The name given by Gomard to the full "throw."
JEU DE L'EPÉE (Fr.). } Fencing with the buttoned sword (*vide*
JEU DE TERRAIN (Fr.). } 'Cold Steel,' p. 127).
JEU DE FLEURET (Fr.). } Foil practice.
JEU DE SALLE (Fr.). }

JOINDRE LE FER (Fr.). } To touch the blade of the opponent with your own, crossing it foible to foible, in order to show that both are ready; any hit given before this has been done is accounted a foul one.
JOIN BLADES, TO. }

JOUR (Fr.). An opening; any part of the person which is not directly covered by the "Guard."

JUSTESSE (Fr.). Precision in the execution of the attack.

LACHÉ (Fr.). } Coup "laché" or "lancé" is the term used by the earlier French writers on Bayonet-fencing to describe the "throw" point in delivering which the left hand quits its hold entirely.
LANCÉ (Fr.). }

LEFT GUARD. The position in Bayonet-fencing which corresponds to that of the left-handed man with the sword.

LEGAMENTO (It.). Engagement.

LINE, TO BE IN. To be directly opposite to the opponent, so that the point of our advanced foot shall be exactly in the direction of the point of his foot.

LINES OF DEFENCE. The four divisions of the body on which, when on guard, we can be attacked; they are :—

LINE, HIGH INSIDE. The division on the left of the sword and above the hilt.

LINE, LOW INSIDE. The division on the left of the sword and below the hilt.

LINE, HIGH OUTSIDE. The division on the right of the sword and above the hilt.

LINE, LOW OUTSIDE. The division on the right of the sword and below the hilt.

In Bayonet-fencing the reverse is the case, the inside being on the right and the outside on the left, for the very simple reason that the left foot is advanced in place of the right foot.

LONGE, OR LUNGE. The extension into the "third" position, which completes the attack by stepping forward with the right foot and keeping the left foot firm.

LOOSE PLAY. (See Assault.)

LOYAL. One who frankly acknowledges the hits he has received.

LUNETTE (Fr.). The twofold ring of metal which forms the guard or shell of the foil.

MAIN GAUCHE (Fr.). The name given to the large "shell" dagger which was carried in the left hand for the purpose of parrying the thrusts of the rapier.

MANCINO (It.). A left-handed person.

MANDRITTI (It.). All cuts given from right to left, i.e., delivered at the left side of the adversary.

MARIER LE JEU (Fr.). To blend the play of two different schools; as, for instance, with the sword, those of the French and the Italians; or with the sabre, those of the modern Italian masters and the English of the 18th century.

MARTINGALE (Fr.). A loop of string by way of a sword-knot, by which the sword is attached to the forefinger in order to prevent being disarmed.

MEDIUM GUARD. Is the guard in sabre or bayonet fencing which is immediately between quarte and tierce.

MENACÉ (Fr.). A feint of a straight thrust.

MESURE (Fr.).
MISURA (It.).   } The space between the combatants as they stand on guard.
MEASURE.

MEASURE, PERFECT. Is when either opponent can when on the lunge touch the body of the other.

MEASURE, OUT OF. When, in order to attack, it is necessary to advance one or more steps.

MEASURE, WITHIN. When either opponent can touch with the extension or "allongement" only.

MISURA STRETTA (It.). (See Corps à corps.)

MONTANTE (It.). A vertical upward cut.

MOULINET (Fr.). A series of exercises of circular cuts, taught in order to afford facility in the use of the sabre, &c. (*vide* 'Cold Steel,' p. 23).

MUR (Fr.). The Academical series of movements which is occasionally performed before commencing the assault.

OCTAVE (Fr.). The eighth parry; it is formed with the nails up and the point depressed; it protects the low outside line.

OCTAVE, HIGH. A parry in sabre play, formed by raising the hilt as high as the head and allowing the point to drop; it defends a riposte delivered over the blade at the right cheek (*vide* 'Cold Steel,' p. 36).

OPPOSITION. Is the closing, during an attack or riposte, of the line on which the opponent's sword lies.

OUT-FIGHTING. } A boxing term; applicable in bayonet play to
OUT-PLAY. } keeping at a distance and using "throws."

OUTSIDE. (See Lines.)

OVER THE SWORD. Another name for the high outside line.

PARADE (Fr.) }
PARATA (IT.). } Is the movement of the weapon which wards off
PARRY. } or stops a thrust or a cut.

PARADES COMPOSÉES (Fr.). (See Compound parries.)

PASS. A full step in advance or retreat, by bringing the rearward foot a complete pace to the front of the advanced foot (*vide* 'Cold Steel,' p. 88), and *vice versâ*.

PASSÉ ! (Fr.). An exclamation used by fencers to denote that an unparried thrust has passed wide of them.

PHRASE D'ARMES (Fr.). The series of attacks, parries, and ripostes exchanged without interruption until a hit is effected.

PLASTRON (FR.). The pad worn by the master when giving a lesson.

PLASTRON DUR (Fr.). A sort of nickname for fencers who do not acknowledge when they are touched.

PLASTRON FIXE (Fr.). The pad which is placed against the wall for the fencers to practise lunging at.

PLASTRONNER (Fr.). To take a fencing lesson.

POIGNÉE (Fr.). The grip or handle of a sword.

PORTÉE (Fr.). Reach.

PRENDERE IL TEMPO (It.) (See Coup de temps.)

PRESSURE.
PRESSION (Fr.). } Leaning slightly with wrist action and "doigté" upon the opponent's blade, in order either to force an opening or draw a response.

PRIME (Fr.). A parry which protects the inside, the point being depressed and the hand in pronation; it was thus named in old times from its being the first position the sword assumed with the point towards the enemy after being drawn from the scabbard.

PRIME, HIGH. Protects the high inside line (*vide* 'Cold Steel,' p. 35).

PRONATION. The position of the hand with the palm and the nails turned downwards.

PUMMEL. The block of iron attached to the end of the hilt, which acts as a counterpoise.

PUMMELLING. Blows with the pummel; these were taught by the masters, even in the 18th century (*vide* 'Cold Steel,' p. 32).

PUNTA DRITTA (It., obs.). A thrust in old rapier play delivered from the right with the hand in pronation.

PUNTA RIVERSA (It., obs.). A thrust in old rapier play delivered from the left with the hand in supination.

PUSH (Obs.). A term signifying a completed thrust.

QUARTE (Fr.). Is the parry which defends the high inside line, by moving the hilt a little to the left, the point being in the upper line and the hand in supination; it was so named in old times from its being accounted the fourth position which the sword assumed after being drawn.

QUARTING (Obs.). (See Volte.)

QUINTE (Fr.). This parry defends the low inside line, the blade nearly horizontal and the hand in moderate pronation. It was regarded as the fifth position of the sword.

RACCOURCI, BRAS (Fr.). The drawing back of the hand in order to avoid a parry and to deliver a stab like the thrust of a poniard. A very great fault.

RADDOPPIO (It.). (See Redouble.)

RALLY. (See Phrase d'armes)

RAPIER. The long cut-and-thrust sword in general use during the 16th and 17th centuries.

RAPIER AND DAGGER. The play of the long rapier supported by a large dagger (main gauche), which was carried in the left hand for the purpose mainly of parrying.

RECEIVE, TO. To act on the defensive and parry the attack.

RECOVER, TO. To spring back to guard after making an attack.

REDOUBLE, TO. To recover instantly after the attack has been parried, and to deliver a second lunge before the enemy has time to riposte.

REMISE (Fr.). A second thrust made on the same lunge without having attempted to first find the opponent's blade.

REPRISE (Fr.). This word has three meanings : 1st, in an assault it is a second thrust made on the same lunge, but after having previously found the opponent's blade ; 2nd, in a treatise on fencing it is a term applied to a series of set lessons, such as " les quatre reprises de Jean Louis " ; 3rd, in a duel it means a series of attacks, parries, and ripostes which occur whether ending in a hit or no.

RETIRE, TO. To move back one or more short paces.

RETRAITE DU BRAS (Fr.). (See Slip.)

RETRAITE DU CORPS (Fr.). To draw back the body without moving the feet from their position, in order to avoid a hit.

RETURN.
RIPOSTE (Fr.). } A hit delivered immediately after having parried the attack.
RISPOSTA (It.).

RETURN, DIRECT. A return given with a simple thrust or cut.

RETURN, COMPOUND.
RIPOSTE COMPOSÉE (Fr.). } A return preceded by a feint.

RITORNO IN GUARDIA (It.). Recovery.

RIVERSI (It.). All cuts given from left to right, i.e., delivered at the right side of the adversary.

ROMPRE (Fr.). To break ground; to retire.

ROUND PARRIES. (See Circles.)

SALUT (Fr.). SALUTE. A movement of courtesy to the spectators and to each other, performed by fencers before commencing the assault.

ST. GEORGE'S PARRY. A parry of the "prime" description, used in sabre play to protect the head (*vide* 'Cold Steel,' p. 38).

SCIABOLATA (It.). A sabre cut.

SCIER LE FER (Fr.). A sawing movement on the opponent's blade, which is made unconsciously by some fencers when on the point of attacking.

SCIOGLIERE LA MISURA (It.). To retire.

SCHERMITORE (It.). A complete swordsman.

SECONDE (Fr.). A parry which protects the low outside line, the point being depressed and the hand in pronation. It received its name in old time from having been the second position in which the sword found itself after having been drawn from the scabbard.

SECONDE, HIGH. A parry of the seconde form, used in sabre play to protect the right side; it was formerly known as the "outside half hanger" (*vide* 'Cold Steel,' p. 38).

SECONDE GUARD, HIGH. An engaging guard in sabre play, in the form of seconde; it is a faulty guard (*vide* 'Cold Steel,' p. 8).

SECONDO COLPO (It.). (See Remise.)

SEIZURE, THE. The act of seizing the person or weapon of the opponent (*vide* 'Cold Steel,' p. 198).

SEMI-CIRCLE (Fr.). SEPTIME (Fr.). The seventh parry in order of nomenclature, which protects the low inside line, the point being depressed and the hand in supination.

SFORZO (It.) (See Froissement.)

SGUALEMBRATO (It., obs.). An oblique downward cut.

SHELL, *or* GUARD. The broad concave plate of metal attached to the hilt to protect the hand.

SINGLESTICK. The ash stick and "bucket" which we use as a cheap substitute for the sabre.

SIXTE (Fr.). The sixth parry in order of nomenclature; it protects the high outside line, and is formed with the point elevated and the hand in supination.

SIXTE, CENTRE. A parry in bayonet-fencing, formed with the centre of the weapon; it defends a cut or a butt stroke at the left side.

SLIP, TO. To draw back the advanced hand or leg when attacked; it is customary to accompany this with a "coup d'arrêt."

SMALL SWORD. The light, triangular, pointed sword worn by all gentlemen in the last century.

SOIE (Fr.). (See Tang.)

STOCCATA (It., obs.). A thrust in rapier fence delivered below the adversary's sword.

STOP-THRUST. "Coup d'arrêt" (*vide* 'Cold Steel,' p. 98).

STRAMAZZONE (It., obs.). A vertical downward cut in rapier fence which is delivered at the head with the part of the weapon close to the point.

SWORD. (Fr. *epée*). The light, triangular, pointed weapon used by The French in their duels. A great many English people, some of whom ought to know better, persist in calling this arm a "rapier"; the rapier became extinct in England and France in the days of Louis XIV.

SUPINATION. The position of the sword-hand with the nails upwards.

TAC AU TAC (Fr.). A term used to demonstrate an instantaneous direct riposte.

TANG. The piece of roughly shaped soft metal at the end of the forte, on to which the grip is fixed.

TARGET. The circular diagram, with cross lines marked on it, used for the practice of the "Moulinets," (*vide* 'Cold Steel,' p. 23). Also, a small round shield (see Buckler).

TEMPO COMMUNE (It.). Is when both combatants lunge at the same time—"coup fourré," in fact.

TIERCE (Fr.). The third parry in order of nomenclature, being, according to the ancients, the third position into which the sword naturally came after having been drawn. It protects the high outside line, and is formed with the point elevated, and the hand in pronation.

TIME THRUST. (See Coup de temps.)

TIRER DE PIED FERME (Fr.). To fence without moving the left foot, to lunge without advancing, and to parry without breaking ground.

TIREUR DANGEREUX (Fr.). A fencer who has been well taught, but who from some natural cause neglects in his assaults the niceties of the academic rules; he uses his brains, and is a puzzling opponent without being a graceful swordsman.

TIREUR DIFFICILE (Fr.). This gentleman emanates usually from a very indifferent school, though he does not think so; he has recourse to all manner of dodges to avoid being hit, such as ducking, twisting his body, jumping about, &c., while in his attacks he tries "remises" "bras raccourcis," and other unconventional methods of scoring a hit. He comes very near to being called a "ferailleur."

TIREUR FORT (Fr.). A swordsman complete in every detail.

TONDI (It., obs.). Horizontal cuts.

TOUCHÉ (Fr.). An exclamation like "à moi," used by loyal fencers in acknowledging a hit.

TOUR D'EPÉE (Fr.). A circle, or rather oval, described around the opponent's blade by passing over his point and under his forte in continuous movement.

TRAVERSE, TO. To effect a lateral change of ground, in order to place the opponent at a disadvantage (*vide* 'Cold Steel,' p. 87).

TROMPER (Fr.). (See Deceive.)

UNDER-QUARTE. A parry in bayonet-fencing, which stops a cut delivered at the right side of the knee (*vide* 'Fixed Bayonets,' p. 78).

UNDER-SIXTE. A parry in bayonet-fencing, which stops a cut at the left side of the knee; the under-sixte also parries, with great force, a thrust at the lower lines (*vide* 'Fixed Bayonets,' p. 77).

UNDER STOP THRUST. The "passata sotto" of the Italians; it is a "coup d'arrêt," effected by sliding back the left foot until the position of the lunge is reached, dropping the body down very low and supporting it by placing the palm of the left hand on the ground; and at the same time receiving the advancing enemy on the point of the sword (*vide* 'Cold Steel,' p. 98).

VOLTE (Fr., obs.). A method of avoiding a thrust by turning about on the toe of the right foot, and at the same time presenting the point to the enemy. The Demi-volte was similarly formed, the body being, as the name indicates, turned only half about; in earlier times this movement was known in England by the name of "quarting," a term derived either from the French "ecarter" or from the Italian "inquartata," a movement which is still in use among the swordsmen of that country.

An adaptation of this Volte is useful to effect a change of front in Bayonet-fencing (*vide* 'Fixed Bayonets,' p. 20).

VOLTE COUPE (Obs.). An attack consisting of a feint above the sword with the nails down, and a thrust under it with the nails up, in the form of Quarte.

YIELDING THE BLADE. (See Ceder l'epée.)

LIST OF WORKS AFFECTING THE BAYONET.

BIBLIOGRAPHICAL LIST OF WORKS AFFECTING THE BAYONET.

*Works marked * are in the possession of the Author.*

ANONYMOUS ENGLISH.

*Manual Exercises for the Rifle and Carbine, and Bayonet Exercise. 32mo, Horse Guards, 1885.

*Physical Drill with Arms, and Bayonet Exercise. Horse Guards, London, 1889, 21 plates out of the text.

ANONYMOUS FRENCH.

Escrime à la baïonnette. (Extrait de l'instruction provis. sur l'exercice et les manœuvres des bataillons de chasseurs à pied.) 32mo, Strasbourg, Levrant, 1842.

[*Translation.*—Bayonet-fencing. (Extract from the provisional instruction in the exercise and manœuvres of the Battalions of "Chasseurs à pied.")]

Un Garde d'Artillerie—" Crosnette.—Une théorie du double jeu de la crosse et de la baionnette." [A theory of the twofold play of the butt and of the bayonet.]

According to Pinette, this work, with drawings, was sent to the Emperor Napoleon about 1811 (?), but was lost sight of in the offices of the Ministry of War.

**Manuscript* by a Belgian Officer. L'escrime du fantassin à la Baionnette. Contains 37 pages of fine clearly-written text; 61 illustrations, of which 10 have been removed, consisting of carefully-drawn pen-and-ink outline figures The writer draws attention to three German works published at Vienna 1819, Dresden 1821, and Stuttgardt 1824, but the titles are not given. Oblong folio, about 1830.

Instruction provisoire sur l'exercice et les manœuvres des bataillons de Chasseurs à pied. Paris, 1841. (Page 100. Cinquième leçon; Escrime à la Baïonnette.)

[*Translation.*—Provisional instruction in the exercise and manœuvres of the battalions of "Chasseurs à pied." (Page 100. Fifth lesson; Bayonet-fencing.)]

On the 22nd July, 1845, this provisional instruction was made. Regulation for the exercise and manœuvres of the battalions of the "Chasseurs d'Orleans," with the same fifth lesson: Bayonet-fencing, page 62, 1st part.

Anonymous German.

Abänderungen zur Instruktion für den Betrieb der Gymnastik und des Bajonetfechtens bei der Infanterie vom 19 Octobr. 1860. Gr. 8vo, Berlin, v. Decker, 1865, 14 woodcuts in the text.

[*Translation.*—Alterations of the Regulations for Gymnastics and Bayonet-fencing for Infantry from 11th October, 1860.]

A work published in Vienna, 1819.

Abrichtungs-Reglement f. d. Kk. Infanterie. Mit 21 Tafeln (nach Gleiger und Kollarz) darstellend d. Bajonettfechten. 8vo, Wien, 1851.

[*Translation.*— Training-rules for the Imperial Infantry. With 21 plates (after Gleiger and Kollarz), illustrative of Bayonet-fencing.]

*Abrichtungs-Reglement f. d. Kk. Pionniere. Mit 17 Tafeln ü. d. Bajonettfechten. 8vo. Wien. 1853.

[*Translation.* — Training-rules for the Imperial pioneers. With 17 plates on Bayonet-fencing.]

Anleitung zum Gebrauch des Bajonets, oder kurzer Unterricht des Wesentlichsten dieser Fechtart, für Unteroffiziere und Soldaten; Dem schweizerischen Fussvolk gewidmet von einem Offizier des eidgenössischen Generalstabs. Basel, 1825.

[*Translation.*—Instruction for the use of the Bayonet, or abridged teaching of the most essential points of this fence, for the use of sub-officers and soldiers. Dedicated to the Swiss Infantry by a Staff Officer of the Confederation.]

Anleitung für Officiere und Unterofficiere beim Ertheilen d. Unterrichts im Turnen und Bajonettiren. 2te nach den allerhöchsten und neuesten Vorschriften bearb. Aufl. von v. B. 16mo, Hanover, Helwing, 1885.

[*Translation.*—Directions for officers and non-commissioned officers when instructing gymnastics and bayonet-fencing.]

Andentungen für den Angriff und die Vertheidigung mit dem Bajonnet, in bestimmten taktischen Verhältnissen. Ein Supplement der bestehenden Vorschriften zur Einübung des Bajonnet-Fechtens. Darmstadt, 1837.

[*Translation.*—Indications for attack and defence with the Bayonet as connected with tactics. A supplement to the existing instructions for Bayonet-fencing.]

A work published in Dresden, 1821.

*Bajonnetir-Reglement für die Groszherz. Hessische Infanterie. Lex. 8vo, Darmstadt, Leske, 1836, 129 pages, 53 plates containing 70 figures.

[*Translation.*—Bayonet rules for the Hessian Grand-ducal Infantry.]

Bajonett-Fecht-Schule in 21 Darstell. mit Erläut. 4to, Hermannstadt, Thierry, 1826.

[*Translation.* — Bayonet-fencing School, in 21 illustrations, with explanations.]

A work published in Stuttgardt, 1824.

*Bajonet-Fechtlehre für die Grossherzogliche badensche Infanterie. 12mo, 55 pages, Mannheim, 1823.

[*Translation.* — Bayonet-fencing Lessons for the Badish Grand-ducal Infantry.]

*Das Bajonettfechten. Leicht faszliche Darstellung, dasselbe in kurzer Zeit gründlich zu erlernen, nebst kurzer Auseinandersetzung, wie solches ohne hohe Kosten in der Schweiz einzuführen. 12mo, Chur, Hitz, 1852, 1 folding plate containing 6 figures, 43 pages.

[*Translation.*—Bayonet-fencing. Simple method to learn it

thoroughly in a short time, with short explanations how it can be introduced, without much cost, into Switzerland.]

*Erste Abhandlung der Bajonet-fechtlehre. 12mo, Karlsruhe, 1823, 44 pages, 6 folding plates.

[*Translation.*—First dissertation on Bayonet-fencing.]

*Gründliche Bajonnet-Fechtschule zur Ausbildung der Lehrer und Vorfechter in der Armee. 8vo, Cassel, Feyschmidt. 15 figures and diagrams in the text, 108 pages, 1863.

[*Translation.*—A thorough School of Bayonet-fencing for educating Instructors and Fencing-masters in the Army.]

Hülfs- und Handbuch f. Offiziere u. Unteroffiziere d. preuss. Infanterie z. Gebrauch bei Ausbildg. d. Mannschaft in d. Gymnastik u. im Bajonet-fechten. 16mo, Potsdam, Döring, 1874.

[*Translation.*—Aide-mémoire and Manual for Officers and N.C. Officers of Prussian Infantry when instructing men in Gymnastics and Bayonet-fencing.]

This little book reached eight editions.

Hülfsbuch für den Infanterie-Unteroffizier zum Gebrauch bei Ausbildung der Mannschaft im Turnen und Bajonettfechten. Zusammengestellt nach den bis 9 Nov. 1882 ergangenen Bestimmgn. 1te u. 2te Aufl. 24mo, Potsdam, Döring, 1884.

[*Translation.*—Aide-mémoire for N.C. Officers of Infantry for use when instructing their men in Gymnastics and Bayonet-fencing. Arranged according to the official regulations issued up to 9th November, 1882.]

Hülfsbuch für den Infanterie-Unteroffizier zum Gebrauch bei Ausbildung der Mannschaft im Turnen und Bajonettfechten. Zusammengestellt nach den Vorschriften uber das Turnen vom 27 Mai 1886, u. das Bajonettfechten vom 9 Novbr. 1882. 4te Auf. 16mo, Potsdam, Döring, 1887.

[*Translation.*—Aide-mémoire for N.C.O.'s of Infantry for perfection in Bayonet-fencing.]

Hülfsbuch zum Betriebe d. Turnens u. d. Bajonettfechtens der Infanterie. Zusammengestellt nach den neuesten Vorschriften zum prakt. Gebrauch und zum Anhalt v. B. 16mo, Torgau, Jacob, 1878.

[*Translation.*—Aide-mémoire for carrying out Gymnastics and

Bayonet-fencing of Infantry. Arranged according to the latest regulations for practical use, and as a guide.]

Instruction über das Bajonetfechten für das K. Preuss. 31 Inf. Regt. 8vo, Erfurt, 1842.

[*Translation.*—Instructions on Bayonet-fencing for the 31st Infantry Regiment Royal Prussian Army.]

*Kriegdienst-Vorschriften für die Grosherzoglich Badischen Truppen XV. Abtheilung. Fünftes Hauptstück. Erste Abschnitt. Bajonet-Fechtunterricht. 8vo, Karlsruhe, 1841, 43 pages, 6 folding plates.

[*Translation.*—Military Regulations for the Troops of the Grand-duchy of Baden, XV. Division. 5th part, 1st chapter: Bayonet-fencing instruction.]

*Praktische Bajonet-Fechtschule auf Grund der Bajonet-Vorschrift für die Infanterie. Vom 15 August, 1889. 12mo, 40 pages, 14 figures in the text, Berlin, 1889.

[*Translation.*—Practical Bayonet-fence School, based on the Bayonet Regulations for the Infantry.]

Praktischer Unterricht in der Bajonetfechtkunst, der schweizerischen Infanterie gewidmet. 8vo, Bern, 1835, 52 figures.

[*Translation.*—Practical instruction in the art of bayonet-fencing, dedicated to the Swiss Infantry.]

Reihenfolge der Kommandswörter f. das Bayonnet-Fechten der königl. bayer. Infanterie. 16mo, München, Kaiser, 1850.

[*Translation.*—The order of the words of command for Bayonet-fencing of the Royal Bavarian Infantry.]

Vorschriften über den Bajonet-Fechtunterricht f. d. Grossh. badenschen Truppen. Carlsruhe, 1841, 6 plates. (*Vide* Kriegdienst.)

[*Translation.*—Regulations on Bayonet-fencing Instruction for the Badish Grand-ducal Troops.]

Vorschriften für den Unterricht im Bayonnet-Fechten der Königl. bayer. Infanterie. 32mo, Amberg, 1843.

[*Translation.*—Regulations for instructing the Royal Bavarian Infantry in Bayonet-fencing.]

*Vorschriften über das Bajonettfechten der Infanterie. 8vo, Berlin, Mittler u. Sohn, 32 pages, 10 figures in the text, 1876.

[*Translation.*—Regulations for Bayonet-exercise of Infantry.]

Vorschriften für das Bajonettfechten der Infanterie. 8vo, Berlin, Mittler u. Sohn, 1882.

[*Translation.*—Regulations for Bayonet-exercise of Infantry.]

Unterrichts-Plan für den Betrieb des gymnastischen Unterrichts auf den königlichen Kriegsschulen, unter zu Grundlegg. der allerhöchst genehmigen Abändergn. und Zusätze zur Instruction für den Betrieb der Gymnastik und des Bajonettfechtens bei der Infanterie vom 19 Octb. 1860. Gr. 8vo, Berlin, v. Decker, 1865.

[*Translation.*—Scheme for the management of Gymnastic instruction in the Royal War-schools, based on the alterations and additions, sanctioned by His Majesty, to the Instruction for the Management for Gymnastics and Bayonet-fencing with Infantry from 19th October, 1860.]

Anonymous Italian.

*Istruzione sulla scherma di Baionetta pei Bersaglieri. 12mo, Firenze, Torino, 1868, 1 folding plate, containing 7 figures, 31 pages.

[*Translation.*—Instruction in Bayonet-fencing for the Bersaglieri.]

*Istruzione per gli esercizi di Ginnastica e di scherma col fucile. 12mo, 1876, 77 pages, the plates do not illustrate Bayonet-fencing.

[*Translation.*—Instructions for the exercises of Gymnastics and Fencing with the Musket.]

Anonymous Russian.

*Начертаніе Правиль Фехтовальнаго Искусства съ рисунками въ пяти частяхъ. Сочиненіе помощника главнаго Фехтовалнаго учителя отдяльнаго гварденскаго корпуса. Соколова. Санктпетербург, 1843, 95 plates, containing 137 figures out of the text.

[*Translation.*—An outline of the rules of fencing, with sketches, in five parts. By the Assistant to the Principal Fencing-master of the separate Corps of Guards. obl. 4to, St. Petersburg, Sokoloff, 1843.]

Anonymous Spanish.

Esgrima de la bayoneta armada, trad. del itaiiano por un Oficial de Milicias Provinciales. Madrid, Leon Amarita, 8vo, 1830.

[*Translation.*—Fencing with the fixed bayonet, translated from the Italian by an Officer of the Provincial Militia.]

ANONYMOUS SWEDISH.

Instruktion i Gymnastik och bajonettfäktning för infanteriet. [Af d. 26 Mars, 1872.]

[*Translation.*—Instruction in Gymnastics and Bayonet-fencing for Infantry.]

*ANGELO. — Bayonet Exercise. 8vo, London, 1829, 39 pages, 12 plates in the text. The first authorised edition appeared in 1857.

D'AZÉMAR.—Combats à la baionnette. Théorie adoptée en 1859 par l'armée d'Italie commandée par l'Empereur Napoléon III. 16mo, Torino, 1859.

[*Translation.*—Combats with the Bayonet. Theory adopted in 1859 by the Army of Italy commanded by the Emperor Napoleon III.]

D'AZÉMAR (Baron) [Obst.]—Theorie der Kämpfe mit dem Bajonett, angenommen im J. 1859 von der italien. Armee unter Napoleon III. aus (des verf.) System der neueren Kriegführg. In's Deutsche übertragen von Lieut. Rich. Stein. Gr. 8vo, Breslau, Kern, 1860.

[*Translation.*—Theory of hand-to-hand fights with the Bayonet, accepted in 1859 by the Italian Army under Napoleon III. from (the author's) System of Modern Warfare. Translated into German by Lieut. Rich. Stein.]

B. (von).—Anleitung für Officiere und Unterofficiere beim Ertheilen d. Unterrichts im Turnen und Bajonettiren. 16mo, Hannover, Helwing, 1881.

[*Translation.*—Directions for Officers and N.C. Officers when instructing Gymnastics and Bayonet-fencing.]

A second edition appeared in 1884, and a third in 1885.

BALASSA, C. K. K. (Major). — Fechtmethode. Eine rationelle, vereinfachte und schnell faszliche Fechtübung des Säbels gegen den Säbel, und dieses gegen das Bajonet und die Picke, zum Hauen, Stechen und Pariren. Eigens für die Cavallerie. nach den aus der Feld- u. Friedens-Praxis geschöpften Grundsätzen in 25 Tabellen, nebst einem kleinen Anhang 'Ueber das Kunstfechten.' Qu. gr. 4to, Pest., 1844, 19 figures.

[*Translation.*—Fencing-method. A rational, simplified, and easily intelligible Fencing-exercise of sabre against sabre, and of sabre against bayonet and pike, for cutting, thrusting, and parrying. Particularly for cavalry, according to the principles gathered from experiences in the field and during peace, in 25 tabulated sheets, together with a small addenda, " On the Art of Fencing."]

BALASSA, C. (Major).—Die militärische Fechtkunst vor dem Feinde. Eine Darstellg. der im Kriege vorkommenden Fechtarten d. Bajonets gegen das Bajonet, d. Säbels gegen den Säbel, u. der Lanze gegen die Lanze, m. Beseitigg. aller beim Kunstfechten vorkommenden, vor dem Feinde aber nicht füglich anwendbaren Stiche, Hiebe u. Paraden zum Gebrauche f. Infanterie u. Kavallerie, m. 26 Abbildgn. nebst e. Anh. über das Kunstfechten m. dem Säbel. Qu. gr. 4to, Pest., Geibel, 1860, 1 lithograph containing 16 figures.

[*Translation.*—The military art of fencing against an enemy. A representation of the modes of fencing on active service, namely: bayonet against bayonet, sabre against sabre, and lance against lance, dismissing all thrusts, cuts, and parries which are used in the art of fencing, but which cannot be employed against an enemy. For use of infantry and cavalry, with 26 illustrations, together with an addenda on the art of fencing with the sabre.]

BURTON, R. F.—A complete system of Bayonet Exercise. 12mo, London, 1853, with 6 plates in the text.

CHAPITRE, F.—Escrime à la Baionnette. 8vo, Bruxelles, 1840 (?).

[*Translation.*—Bayonet-fencing.]

*A second edition, slightly altered, appeared in 1872. 48 pages, 23 plates out of the text.

*CHATIN (LE CAPITAINE).—Escrime à la Baionnette. [Bayonet-fencing.] 12mo, Paris, 1856, 21 pages, 24 figures out of the text.

Christmann und Pfeffinger. Theoret.-praktische Anleitung des Hau-Stossfechtens und des Schwadronhauens nach einen ganz neuen methode, nebst einen Anhange: 'Verbalten des Degen-oder Säbelführenden gegen der Bajonnetisten, &c.' 8vo, 1838, 192 pages 12 plates containing 119 figures out of the text.

[*Translation.*—Theoretical and practical directions for point-fencing, &c., on an entirely new method, including a supplement: 'Action of the Swordsman or Sabreur against the Bayoneteer.'

*COLE, BENJAMIN.—The Soldier's Pocket Companion; or, the Manual Exercise of our British Foot as now practis'd by his Majesty's special command; with previous Directions to Officers in regard to their proper Salutes to the King, or any other of the Royal Family, &c. To which is added a Short View of the Use of the Small-sword. 8vo, 1746, London, 96 pages, 96 plates out of the text.

*ELLIOTT, Major W. J. (late of H.M. War Department).—The Art of Attack and Defence in use at the present time. Fencing: Sword against Sword or Bayonet (Singlestick); Bayonet against Sword or Bayonet; Boxing. 8vo, London, Dean and Son, 1884, 61 figures in the text, of which only 9 in any way relate to the Bayonet.

FELDMANN, JOS. (Major).—Leitfaden zum Unterrichte im Rappier-, Säbel-, Bajonet- und Stockfechten. Gr. 8vo, Wiener-Neustadt, Lentner, 1882.

[*Translation*.—Guide to instruct in Fencing with Singlestick, Rapier, Sword, and Bayonet.]

*A second edition appeared in 1886. 116 pages, 56 plates containing 77 figures out of the text.

FRANCKENBERG-LUDWIGSDORFF, M. VON.—Das Bajonetfechten. Nach den Grundsäten der neueren Zeit umgeändert. 8vo, Münster, Wundermann, 1845, 6 copper plates.

[*Translation*.—Bayonet-fencing. Altered according to the principles of modern times.]

*FRANCKENBERG-LUDWIGSDORFF, Hauptm. von.—Betrachtungen über das Bajonettfechten und den bisherigen Betrieb desselben in der Armee. Ein Vortrag gehalten zur Anregg. der Besprechung im Officier-Corps. 12mo, Berlin, Mittler u. Sohn, 20 pages, 1861.

[*Translation*.—Considerations on Bayonet-fencing, and how it has been carried out hitherto in the Army. A lecture held with the object of discussing the questions in the Officer Corps.

GALVEZ DE ZEA, Don Francisco.—Esgrima de la bayoneta. 8vo, Valencia, 1855, 16 figures.

[*Translation*.—Bayonet-fencing.]

*GOMARD.—See Posselier.

*GORDON, ANTHONY.—A Treatise on the Science of Defence for the Sword, Bayonet, and Pike, in close action. 4to, London, 1805, 19 plates. This is the earliest known work giving any idea of attack and defence with the bayonet.

HEINZE, A. C.—Katechismus der Bajonetfechtkunst. 8vo, Leipzig, Weber, 1851.

[*Translation.*—Catechism of Bayonet-fencing.]

*HUTTON, A.—Swordsmanship. Written for the members of the Cameron Fencing Club, by Lieut. A. Hutton, Her Majesty's Cameron Highlanders. 8vo. Simlah, 1862, 11 pages.

*HUTTON, A.—Swordsmanship, for the use of Soldiers. 8vo, London, W. Clowes and Sons, 1866, 16 pages.

*HUTTON, ALFRED (Lieut. King's Dragoon Guards).—Swordsmanship and Bayonet-fencing. 8vo, London, W. Clowes and Sons, 1867, 24 pages.

*HUTTON, ALFRED.—Bayonet-fencing and Sword-practice, by Alfred Hutton, late Captain King's Dragoon Guards. 8vo, London, W. Clowes and Sons, 1882, 31 pages.

*HUTTON, ALFRED.—Cold Steel: a Practical Treatise on the Sabre. Based on the Old English Backsword Play of the Eighteenth Century, combined with the Method of the Modern Italian School; also on various other weapons of the present day, including the Short Sword-Bayonet and the Constable's Truncheon. By Alfred Hutton, late Captain King's Dragoon Guards; author of 'Swordsmanship,' 'Bayonet-fencing and Sword-practice,' &c. 8vo. cloth, 10s. 6d., illustrated with numerous figures, and also with reproductions of engravings from masters of bygone years. Imperial 8vo, London, 1889, 245 pages, frontispiece, and 55 plates out of the text.

*HUTTON, ALFRED.—Fixed Bayonets. A complete system of Fence for the British Magazine Rifle, explaining the uses of point, edges, and butt, both in offence and defence; comprising also a Glossary of English, French, and Italian terms common to the art of Fencing, with a Bibliographical List of Works affecting the Bayonet. Imperial 8vo, London, 1890, 175 pages, frontispiece, and 23 illustrations out of the text.

JENSEN.—Die Anwendung des Bajonets gegen Infanterie und Kavallerie in d. königl.-Dänischen Armee (aus d. Dänischen übertragen von den Kapitän v. Jensen). 12mo, Braunschweig, Vieweg, 1829.

[*Translation.* — The employment of the Bayonet against Infantry and Cavalry in the Danish Royal Army, translated from the Danish by Captain v. Jensen.]

LANCKE, JUL. (Prem. Lieut.).—Praktische Anleitung zur Ausbildung und Vorstellung der II. Bajonetfechtklasse. Nach den Vorschriften über das Bajonetfechten der Infanterie aus dem J. 1876 und eigenen Erfahrgn. zusammengestellt. 8vo, Mainz, V. von Zabern, 1878.

[*Translation.*—Practical directions for instructing and inspecting the Second Bayonet-fencing Class. Arranged according to the official regulations and as suggested by own experience.]

LEMOINE, AL.—Traité d'éducation physique, comprenant la natation, l'escrime à la baionnette, la boxe française, l'escrime à l'épée, la gymnastique. Gr. in-8, Gand, 1857, with an atlas of 56 plates.

[*Translation.*—Treatise on Physical Education, comprising Swimming, Bayonet-fencing, French Boxing, Foil-fencing, and Gymnastics.]

*LINSINGEN, A. von—Handbuch zur Anweisung des Soldaten in der Gymnastik und im Bajonetfechten. 108 pages, 5 folding plates containing 30 figures. 8vo, Hannover, 1854.

[*Translation.*—Handbook of instructions of the Soldier in Gymnastics and Bayonet-fencing.]

*MCCLELLAN, GEORGE B.—Manual of Bayonet Exercise: prepared for the use of the Army of the United States. 8vo, Philadelphia, 1862, 118 pages, 24 plates containing 58 figures out of the text.

MARIN, Don ANTONIO.—Esgrima á la bayoneta, ó manejo de dicha arma aplicado á los ejercicios y maniobras de la infantería aprobado por S. M. y mandado observar por Real órden de 13 de setiembre de 1859. Traducido del francés de Th. Pinette. Cadiz, 1859, 3 plates.

[*Translation.*—Bayonet-fencing, or the management of that arm applied to the exercises and manœuvres of Infantry, approved by H.M. and ordered to be observed by Royal Command, September 13, 1859. Translated from the French of Th. Pinette.]

*Mathewson, T. (Lieutenant and Riding Master in the late Roxbrough Fencible Cavalry).—Fencing Familiarised, or a new treatise on the art of the Scotch broadsword, showing the superiority of that weapon when opposed to an enemy armed with a spear, pike, or gun and bayonet. 8vo, Salford, printed by W. Cowdray, jun., 1805, 13 plates out of the text.

Merelo y Casademunt, D. Jaime (Profesor de esgrima en el colegio de infantería).—Tratado de la verdadera esgrima del fusil ó carabina armados de bayoneta. 4to, Toledo, J. Lopez Fando, 1858, 2 plates.

[*Translation.*—Treaties on the true Fence of the Musket or Carabine furnished with the Bayonet.]

*Merelo y Casademunt, Don Jaime.—Elementos de esgrima para instruir al soldado de infantería en la verdadera destreza del fusil ó carabina armados de bayoneta. 12mo, Toledo, 80 pages, 3 folding plates containing 17 figures. 1865.

[*Translation.*—Elements of Fencing, to instruct the infantry soldier in the true art of Fencing with Musket or Carabine with fixed bayonet.]

Montret (Sous officier du 12ᵉ Léger) " est l'auteur du premier traité qui ait été fait sur le sujet dont nous vous occupons. Ce traité contenait plûtot des exercices pour le maniement du bâton que pour l'escrime à la baionnette."—*Pinette.*

[*Translation.*—" is the author of the first treatise which has been written on the subject with which we are now occupied. This treatise contained more exercises for the management of the 'Great Stick' than for Bayonet-fencing."] It apparently did not get beyond the MS. stage. 1811 (?).

Muller, Al.—Maniement de la baïonnette appliqué à l'attaque et à la défense de l'infanterie. 4to, Paris, 1835, 20 plates.

[*Translation.*—The Management of the Bayonet as applied to the attack and defence of infantry.]

Muller, Alessandro.—Il maneggio della baionetta all' attacco ed alla difesa, &c. ... con 53 figure. Traduzione italiana dalla 2ª francese del 1835. 8vo, Torino, 1835.

[*Translation.*—The Management of the Bayonet in attack and defence, &c., with 53 figures.]

*MÜLLER, A. (Capitaine)—Maniement de la Baionnette. [*Management of the Bayonet.] 24mo, 1845, 44 pages, 31 figures in the text.

MÜLLER, FRZ.—Fecht-Unterricht mit dem Feuer-Gewehre, eigentlich Bajonetfechten. Kl. 8vo, Prag., Haase Söhne, 1841, 6 lithographs.

[*Translation.*—Lessons in Fencing with the Infantry Fire-arm; really, Bayonet-exercise.]

NYBLŒUS, GUSTAF. Öfningstabeller till ledning för undervisningen i gymnastik och bajonettfaktning vid indelta arméns korprals- och volontärskolor. På anmodan af statsrådet och chefen för Kongl. landtförsvarsdepartementet utarbetade. 8vo, Stockholm, Norstedt & Söners, 1887.

[*Translation.*—Tables for learning Gymnastics and Bayonet-fencing.]

*PINETTE, JOSEPH.—École du tirailleur, ou maniement de la baionnette appliqué aux exercices et manœuvres de l'infanterie. 24mo, Paris, Dumaine, 1832, 108 pages, 22 figures in a folding plate.

[*Translation.*—School of the Skirmisher, or management of the Bayonet applied to the exercises and manœuvres of Infantry.]

This book went into eight editions, the last of which appeared in 1846, besides a translation into Spanish. See Marin.

PINETTE, JOSEPH.—Théorie de l'escrime à la baionnette. 18mo, Paris, Dumaine, 1847, 16 figures.

[*Translation.*—Theory of Bayonet-fencing.]

*PINETTE, JOSEPH.—Réfutation de l'escrime à la baionnette de M. Gomard. 8vo, Paris, Dumaine, 1847, 42 pages.

[*Translation.* — Refutation of the Bayonet-fencing of M. Gomard.]

PINETTE. J.—Katechismus der Bayonnetfechtkunst. 8vo, Leipzig, 1851, 16 figures.

[*Translation.*—Catechism of Bayonet-fencing.]

*PINETTE, J.—Dissertation sur l'emploi de la Baionnette, &c. Par Joseph Pinette. 8vo, Montrouge, 1860.

[*Translation.*—Dissertation on the employment of the Bayonet, &c.]

*Possellier, A. J. J. (dit Gomard).—L'Escrime à la baionnette, ou Ecole du fantassin pour le maniement du fusil comme arme blanche. 8vo, Paris, 1847, 208 pages, 36 plates containing 67 figures.

    [*Translation.*—Bayonet-fencing, or School of the Infantry Soldier for the Musket treated as cold steel.]

Quehl, F. W.—Anweisung zum Bayonetfechten. 8vo, Berlin, 1866.

    [*Translation.*—Directions for Bayonet-fencing.]

R., (Hauptm.) v.—Anleitung zum Kontrabajonettfechten im Anschusz an den Entwurf der provisorischen Vorschriften für das Bajonettfechten der Infanterie. 12mo, Berlin, Siebel, 1882.

    [*Translation.*—Directions for Bayonet-fencing, based on the synopsis of the provisional regulations for Bayonet-exercise for Infantry.]

Rothstein, H.—Des Bajonetfechten nach dem System P. H. Ling's reglementarisch dargestellt (auf 2 Steintaf. in qu. fol.). 12mo, Berlin, Schroeder, 1853, 2 folding plates containing 32 figures, 72 pages.

    [*Translation.*—Bayonet-fencing according to P. H. Ling's system, put in regulation form (on 2 plates in qu. fol.).]

    *A second edition appeared in 1860, and a third in 1872.

Rothstein, H.—Anleitung zum Bajonetfechten. 1te u. 2te unveränd. Abdr. 12mo, Berlin, Schroeder, 1853, 1 plate containing 11 figures, 19 pages.

    [*Translation.*—Directions for Bayonet-fencing, first and second unaltered edition.]

    *Another edition appeared in 1857.

*Rhein, A. von.—Das Bajonetfechten. 8vo, Wesel, 1840, 51 pages, 1 plate out of the text, and 7 folding plates giving 35 figures.

    [*Translation.*—Bayonet-fencing.]

*Rhein, A. von.—Das Bajonetfechten. 2te Aufl. Wesel, 1844, 37 pages, 19 plates, giving 35 figures out of the text.

Rücker (Prem. Lieut.).—Vergleichung der Bajonnettfechtens der preuszischen und französischen Armee. 16mo, Luxemburg, Heintze, 1865, 9 lithographed plates.

    [*Translation.*—Comparison of the Prussian and French Bayonet-exercise.]

SCORZA, Il Barone ROSAROLL. — Scherma della baionetta astata. 8vo, Napoli, 1818.

[*Translation.*—Fencing with the fixed bayonet.]

SELMNITZ, ED. von (Ritter).—Die Bajonettfechtkunst, oder Lehre des Verhaltens mit d. Infanterie-Gewehre als Angriffs- und Vertheidigungswaffe. 1er Theil. 8vo, Dresden, 1825, 10 folio copper plates and 1 vignette.

A second edition appeared in 1831, and a *third in 1832. The third edition has 167 pages, and 10 folding plates containing 31 figures.

*SELMNITZ.—De l'escrime à la baionnette, ou instruction pour l'emploi du fusil d'infanterie comme arme d'attaque et de défense; par Selmnitz, capitaine de l'armée saxonne. Traduit de l'allemand par J. B. N. Merjay, officier de l'armée belge. Paris et Bruxelles, s.d. (1840), 8vo, 174 pages, avec 4 planches contenant 12 figures.

[*Translation.*—Bayonet-fencing, or instruction for the use of the Infantry Musket as an arm of attack and defence; by Selmnitz, a Captain in the Saxon Army. Translated from the German by J. B. N. Merjay, an officer of the Belgian army.]

S. (v.)—Hülfsbuch zum Betriebe der Gymnastik u. d. Bajonetfechtens für Offiziere und Unteroffiziere der preuszisch-norddeutschen Infanterie. 2te u. 3te Aufl. 32mo, Nordhausen, Eick, 1870.

[*Translation.*—Aide-mémoire for Officers and Non-Commissioned Officers of the Prussian and North German Infantry when practising Gymnastics and Bayonet-fencing.] The 16th edition appeared in 1890.

SINNER. — Praktischer Unterricht in der Bajonetfechtkunst, der schweizerischen Infanterie gewidmet. 8vo, Bern and Chur, 52 figures, 1835.

[*Translation.*—Practical Instruction in Bayonet-fencing, dedicated to the Swiss Infantry.]

SPINAZZI, PIETRO.—Il bersagliere in campagna ed istruzione sulla scherma della baionetta, corredato di tavole dimostrative. Genova, 1851.

[*Translation.*—The Marksman in the Field; and instruction in Bayonet-fencing, enriched with descriptive plates.]

STJERNSVARD, G. M.—Handbok uti Gymnastik och Bajonett-Fäktning. 24mo, Stockholm, 1843, 2 plates.
[*Translation.*—Handbook of Gymnastics and Bayonet-fencing.]

STOCKEN, HAUPTM. — Uebungs-Tabellen für den systematischen Betrieb der Gymnastik und des Bajonnetfechtens bei der Infanterie. 1te u. 2te Aufl. Berlin, Schroeder, 1862.
[*Translation.*—Exercise-tables for systematically practising Gymnastics and Bayonet-fencing with Infantry.]
A third edition appeared in 1864, and a fourth in 1867.

THALHOFER UND ISNARDI. — Theoret.-praktische Anleitung zur Fechtkunst à la Contrepointe. Nebst einem Anleitung zur Vertheidigung mit d. Säbel oder Degen der Bajonnetisten von Thalhofer. Mit 1 Heft figuren. Gr. 8vo, Wien, 59 plates. 1838.
[*Translation.*—Theoretical and practical directions for defence with Sabre or Sword against the Bayoneteer.]

*TÖRHGREN, L. M.—Reglemente i bajonett- och sabelfäktning för kongl. flottan. Enligt nädigt uppdrag utarbetadt. 12mo, Stockholm, Norstedt & Söner, 1882, 148 pages, 21 plates containing 23 figures out of the text.
[*Translation.*—Regulations for Bayonet and Sabre Practice in the Royal Navy. Composed with gracious permission.]

TÖRNGREN, L. M.—Tilläggsblad för reglemente i bajonett och sabelfäktning. (Omslagstitel: Supplement för Atlas till gymnastik reglemente för kongl. flottau.) Folio, Stockholm, Norsted & Söner, 1882, 6 plates.
[*Translation.*—Addendum to Regulations for Bayonet and Sabre Play. (Title on wrapper: Supplement to Atlas for Gymnastic Regulations for the Royal Navy.)]

*WAITE, J. M. (Professor of Fencing, late 2nd Life Guards.)—Lessons in Sabre, Singlestick, Sabre and Bayonet, and Sword Feats; or, how to use a cut-and-thrust sword. 8vo, London, Weldon & Co., 1880, with 34 plates.

WAITE, J. M.—Sword and Bayonet-exercise. *n. d.*

*WECK, C. R. A. — Bajonett-fechtinstruction, für die königlich Preussiche Infanterie; bearbeitet von C. R. A. Weck, Unteroffizier im 36 Infanterie-Regiment. 8vo, Mainz, 1836, 92 pages, 5 folding plates containing 46 figures.

[*Translation.*—Instruction in Bayonet-fencing, for the use of the Royal Prussian Infantry. Composed by C. R. Weck, Under-officer in the 36th Regiment of Infantry.]

WEISS, GIUSEPPE.—Scherma della baionetta. 4to, Neapoli, 1830.

[*Translation.*—Bayonet-fencing.]

WIELAND, JH.—Anleit. zum Gebrauch des Bajonets oder kurzer Unterricht des Wesentlichsten dieser Fechtkunst. 8vo, Basel, Schweighäuser, 1826.

[*Translation.*—Directions for the use of the Bayonet; or, short instructions for what is most important in this art of Fencing.]

CHRONOLOGICAL ORDER OF AUTHORS OF WORKS ON THE BAYONET.

1746. *Cole, B.
1800.
1801.
1802.
1803.
1804.
1805. *Anthony Gordon.—*Mathewson, of Salford.
1806.
1807.
1808.
1809.
1810.
1811 (about).   Montret.—Un Garde d'Artillerie.
1812.
1813.
1814.
1815.
1816.
1817.
1818. Scorza.
1819. A German work published in Vienna.
1820.
1821. A German work published in Dresden.
1822.
1823. *Anonymous German, published at Mannheim.—*Anonymous German, published at Karlruhe.
1824. A German work published at Stuttgardt.
1825. *Selmnitz.—Anonymous German, published at Basel.
1826. Anonymous German, published at Hermanstadt.—Wieland.
1827.
1828.

1829. Jensen.—*Angelo.
1830. Weiss. — Anonymous Spanish, published in Madrid.—*French M.S.
1831.
1832. *Pinette.
1833.
1834.
1835. Muller, A.—Muller, A.—Sinner.
1836. *Anonymous German, published in Darmstadt.—*Weck.
1837. Anonymous German, published in Darmstadt.
1838. *Christmann und Pfeffinger.—Thalhofer und Isnardi.
1839.
1840. Anonymous French, published at Strasbourg.—*Chapitre.—*Von Rhein.—*Selmnitz-Merjay.
1841. Anonymous French, published in Paris.—Anonymous German, published in Carlsruhe.—Muller, Frz.
1842. Anonymous German, published at Erfurt.
1843. *Anonymous Russian, published at St. Petersburg.—Anonymous German, published at Amberg.—Stjernsvard.
1844. *Von Rhein.—Balassa.
1845. Franckenstein-Ludwigsdorf.—*Muller, A.
1846.
1847. Pinette.—*Pinette.—*Possellier.
1848.
1849.
1850. Anonymous German, published at Munchen.
1851. Heinze.—Pinette.—Spinazzi.—*Anonymous German, published in Vienna.
1852. *Anonymous German, published at Chur.
1853. Burton, R. F. — *Rothstein. — *Rothstein. — *Anonymous German, published in Vienna.
1854. *Von Linsingen.
1855. Galves de Zea.
1856. *Chatin.
1857. Lemoine.
1858. Merelo y Casademunt.
1859. d'Azemar.—Marin.
1860. d'Azemar.—*Pinette. Balassa.

1861. *Franckenstein-Ludwigsdorf.
1862. *Hutton, A.—*McClellan.—Stocken.
1863. *Anonymous German, published at Cassel.
1864.
1865. Anonymous German, published in Berlin.—*Merelo y Casademunt.—Rucker.
1866. *Hutton, A.—Quehl.—Anonymous German, published in Berlin.
1867. *Hutton, A.
1868. *Anonymous Italian, published in Turin.
1869.
1870. Von S.
1871.
1872. Anonymous Swedish, published in Stockholm.
1873.
1874. Anonymous German, published at Potsdam.
1875.
1876. *Anonymous Italian.—*Anonymous German, published in Berlin.
1877.
1878. Anonymous German, published at Torgau.—Lancke.
1879.
1880. *Waite.
1881. Von B.
1882. *Hutton, A.—*Anonymous German, published in Berlin.—*Feldmann.—Von R.—*Törngren.—Törngren.
1883.
1884. Anonymous German, published at Potsdam.—*Elliott, W. J.
1885. *Anonymous English, published in London.—Anonymous German, published in Hanover.
1886.
1887. Anonymous German, published in Potsdam.—Nyblœus.
1888.
1889. *Anonymous English, published in London.—*Hutton, A.—*Anonymous German, published in Berlin.
1890. *Hutton, A.
N.D. Waite.

INDEX.

ABÄNDERUNGEN zur Instruction, &c., 158
s'Abandonner, 135
Aborder, 135
About, 6, 25
Abrichtungs-Reglement, 158,
—— ——, 158,
Absence, 135
Academical, 135
Accidental pressure, 118
Acknowledge, 117
Advance, To, 135
Advanced hand, 78, 89
—— lessons, 51
Adversaire, 135
Affondo, 135
Against the Long Bayonet, 131
Aldershot Gymnasium, 3, 9
Aller à l'epée, 135
Allonge, The, 27
Allongement, 135
À moi, 135
Andeutungen für den Angriff, &c, 159
Angelo, 2, 4, 5, 35, 163, 174
——'s Bayonet-exercise, 2, 163
——'s School of Arms, 1
Anleitung für Officiere, &c., 159
—— zum Gebrauch, 158
Annoncer, 135
Appât, 135
Appel, 135
Appuntata, 136
Arresto, Colpo di, 136
Assaillant, 136

Assault, 117, 136
Assaut, 136
Assalto, 136
Assault of Arms, 136
Assaut d'Armes, 136
Attack, Simple, 136
——, Compound, 136
——, Single and Double, 136
Attacks on the weapon, 52
Avoir des Jambes, 136
—— de la Main, 136
—— —— Tête, 136
—— une parade, &c., 136
d'Azemar, 163, 175

B., Von, 163, 176
Back Butt-thrust, 71
Backsword, 136
Bajonet-Fechtlehre, 159
—— -Fechtschule, 159
Bajonnettir-Reglement, 159
Balance, 19
Balassa, 163, 164, 175
Basket, 137
—— -hilt, 137
Battement, 137
—— sec., 53
Battuta, 137
Bayonet against Sabre, 125
'—— Exercise' (New), v., 1–10, 119
—— -fencing, 137
'—— -fencing and Sword Practice, vi., 4, 13, 40, 93, 137, 166
Beat, The, 10, 53, 137
Bersaglio, 137

N

INDEX.

Binding, 137
Blindfold lessons, 137
Bondir, 137
Botte, 137
Botta dritta, 137
Bout, 137
Bouton, 137
Bras raccourci, 5, 137
Break ground, 138
Bretteur, 138
British Magazine Rifle, i.
Broadsword, 138
Brocchiero, 138
Brush, 138
Bucket, 138
Buckler, 138
Burton, R. F., iv., 164, 175
Butt, 14, 77, 78
—— -fencing, 17, 93-113
—— -thrust, 71
Button, 138

CAMBIARE, 138
Cameron Fencing Club, 13
Capot, Faire, 138
Capotto, Dar, 138
Captif, 138
Captive, 138
Captiver, 138
Castle, Mr. Egerton, iii.
Caveating, 138
Cavazione, 138
Caver, 138
Ceder l'Epée, 138
Centre, 18, 72, 77, 78, 87, 96, 109, 139
Centre of percussion, 13
Centre-quarte, 87
Centre-sixte, 87
Change, 139
"Change Arms," 6
Change of engagement, 36
Change guard, 23
Changer, 139
Chapitre, vi., 94, 164, 175
Chasse-coquin, 139

Chasser les mouches, 139
Chatin, M. le Capitaine, vi. 28, 164, 175
Christmann u. Pfeffinger, 164, 175
Circles, 139
'Cold Steel,' iii. 6, 25, 67, 93
Cole, Benjamin, 165, 174
Combinations, 139
—— (on point), 61-63.
—— (edge and point), 88, 89
—— (Butt-fencing), 110, 111
—— (Right Guard v. Left Guard), 112, 113
Command, To, 6, 139
Compound attacks, 139
—— parries, 139
—— ripostes, 55
Contraction, 139
Contres, 139
Contri, 139
Contre dégagement, 140
Contro-cavazione, 140
Counters, 139
Counter disengagement, 140
Corps à corps, 140
Coucher, Se, 140
Coulé, 140
Counter-time, 140
—— -hit, 140
—— caveating, 140
Coup, 140
—— d'arrêt, 140
—— de banderole, 140
—— —— bouton, 140
—— composé, 140
—— de crosse en arrière, 71
—— droit, 140
—— d'epée, 140
—— de figure, 140
—— de flanc, 140
—— de Jarnac, 68, 140
—— lâché, 35
—— lancé, 35
—— de manchette, 140
—— passé, 141

Coup de sabre, 140
—— simple, 141
—— de temps, 141
—— —— tête, 140
—— —— ventre, 140
Couper, 141
Coups fourrés, 141
Court sword, 141
Couvert, 141
Covered, 141
Critical Remarks, &c., 1–10
Croisé, 141
Croiser, Se, 141
"Crosnette" (un Garde d'Artillerie, 157
Coward's guard, 141
Cudgelling, 141
Cut 1, 68
—— 2, 68
—— 3, 68
—— 4, 68
—— 5, 68
—— 6, 68
—— over, 39, 141

DAS Bajonettfechten, 159
Deceive, 141
Decoller, Se, 141
Decouvert, 141
Dedans, 142
Deflecting the point, 9
Dégagement, 142
Déhors, 142
Dérober, 142
Dérobement, 36
Désarmer, 142
Dessous, 142
Dessus, 142
Detente, 142
Développement, 142
Disengage, 142
Disengagement, 36
Disordinata, 142
Distance, 142

Doigté, 142
Donner le fer, 142
Doubler, 142
Droitier, 142

s'EBRANLER, 142
Ecarter, 142
Ecole du fantassin, 117, 169
Edges, The, 14, 67
s'Effacer, 142
Elasticity, 19
Elliott, Major, 165, 176
"Engage," 3, 8
Engagement, 142
Enfield Muzzle-loader, v.
Epée, 143
Epée de salle, 143
Erste Abhändlung, &c., 160
Escrime, 143
Escrime à la baionnette, 157
l'Escrime du fantassin, 157
Escrimeur, 143
Esgrima de la bayoneta, 162
Espadon, 143
Eviter, 143
Exchanged hits, 143
Extension, 143

FAIRE des Armes, 143
False attack, 143
—— edge, 14, 143
—— guard, 143
Falso dritto, 143
—— manco, 143
Fausse attaque, 143
Feeling, 143
Feints, 54–59, 143
Feldmann, 165, 176
Fendre, Se, 144
Fencing, 144
Fendente, 144
Ferailleur, 144
Fianconnata, 144
Figure of Eight, 144

Filo di Spada, 144
Finta, 144
"First Point," 3
—— Position, 144
Fixed Bayonets, 13, 166
Flançonnade, 144
Fleuret, 144
Flexibility of limb, 40
Flying Point, 144
Foible, 9, 17, 144
Forconare, 144
Forte, 17, 41, 109, 144
Foul blow, 144
Frankenburg-Ludwigsdorf, 165, 175, 176
Frase, 144
Froissement, 144
Frolé, 144
"Fulcrum," 8, 26
Fuor di presenza, 67, 144

GALVEZ DE ZEA, 165, 175
Game of the Sword, 145
Gaucher, 145
Glisse de l'arme, 28, 145
Glizade, 145
Gomard, vi. 4, 28, 71, 106
Gordon, Captain Anthony, iv., 166, 174
"Grasp his thigh," 4, 7
Great Stick, The, 23, 26, 145
Gründliche Bayonnet-fechtschule, 160
Guard, 145
Garde, 145
Guardia, 145
Guard, The, 18
——, The Resting, 20
"——, Third," 9
—— (in Butt-fencing), 95
"Guards, First and Second," 8
Guard, To, 145
Guider, Se, 145

HALF Circle, 145
Heintze, 166, 175
Helmet, 145
Henry-Martini Rifle, v.
High lines, 145
Horizontal quarte, 78
—— prime, 87
Hülfsbuch für den Infanterie, 160
—— —— —— ——, 160
Hülfsbuch zum Betriebe, 160
Hülfs und Handbuch, 160
Hutton, A., 165, 166, 176

IMBROCCATA, 145
Incito, 145
Incontro, 145
In-fighting, 145
In play, 145
Inquartata, 145
Instruction provisoire, 158
—— über das Bajonetfechten, &c. 160
Instruktion i Gymnastik och B., &c., 162
Istruzione sulla scherma, &c., 162
—— per gli esercizi, &c., 162

JENSEN, 166, 175
Jet de l'arme, 35, 146
Jeu de l'epée, 146
—— de fleuret, 146
—— de salle, 146
—— de terrain, 146
Joindre le fer, 146
Join blades, To, 146
Jour, 146
Justesse, 146

K. D. G. School, 4
Krieg-dienst Vorschriften, &c., 161

LÂCHÉ, 146
Lancé, 146

Lancke, 167, 176
Left Guard, 24, 146
Legamento, 146
Lemoine, 167, 175
Line, To be in, 146
——, high inside, 40, 146
——, low inside, 26, 40, 146
——, high outside, 40, 146
——, low outside, 26, 40, 146
Lines of attack, 26
—— of defence, 40, 146
Linsingen, Von, 167, 175
Longe, or "Lunge," The, 6, 147
Loose play, 147
Loyal, 147
Lunette, 147

MAIN Gauche, 147
Mancino, 147
Mandritti, 147
Manual Exercises, &c., 157
Marier le jeu, 147
Marin, 167, 175
Mathewson, 167, 174
McClellan, iv., 167, 176
Martingale, 147
Medium Guard, 19, 147
Menacé, 147
Merelo y Casademunt, 168, 175, 176
Measure, 147
——, Perfect, 147
——, Out of, 147
——, Within, 147
Mesure, 147
Misura, 147
—— stretta, 147
Montante, 147
Montret, 168, 174
Moulinet, 148
Muller, Alexandre, 168, 169, 175
Müller, Frz., 169, 175
Mur, 148

NYBLŒUS, 169, 176

OCTAVE, 148
——, High, 148
Opposition, 148
Out-fighting, 148
Out-play, 148
Outside, 148
Over the sword, 148
Overbalanced posture, 7

PADDED butts, 94
Parade, 148
Parata, 148
Parry, 148
Parades composées, 148
Parries, 40
——, Supplementary, 72
—— in Butt-fencing, 96, 109
Pass, 148
Passé! 148
Pelvis, 8
Phrase d'armes, 148
"Physical Drill, &c.," 1, 157
Pinette, 169, 175
Plastron, 148
Plastron dur, 148
Plastron fixe, 148
Plastronner, 149
"Plate M.," 5
"Plate S.," 9
Poignée, 149
Point, The, 14, 26
Portée, 149
Possellier, 170, 175
Praktische Bayonetfechtschule, 161
—— Unterricht, 161
Prendere il tempo, 149
Pression, 149
Pressure, 53, 149
——, Involuntary, 118
Prime, 72, 149
—— High, 149
Prime-thrust, 28
Pronation, 149
Prove distance, 27

Pummel, 149
Pummelling, 149
Punta dritta, 149
—— riversa, 149
Push, 149

QUARTE, 40, 41, 149
—— line, 26
—— medium, 19
Quarting, 149
Quehl, 170, 176
Quinte, 149

R., Von, 170, 176
Raccourci, Bras, 5, 150
Raddoppio, 150
Rally, 150
Rapier, 150
—— and dagger, 150
Receive, To, 150
Recover, To, 150
Redouble, 150
Reihenfolge der Kommandswörter, &c., 161
Remise, 67, 150
Reprise, 150
Resting Guard, The, 20
Resting medium, The, 20
Retire, To, 150
Retraite du bras, 150
—— du corps, 150
Return, 150
—— direct, 150
—— compound, 150
Rhein, Von, 170, 175
Riposte, 51, 150
—— composée, 150
Risposta, 150
Ritornio in Guardia, 150
Riversi, 150
Rompre, 151
Rothstein, 170, 175
Round parries, 151

Rucker, 170, 176
Russian anonymous work, 162

S., Von, 171, 176
Salut, 151
Salute, 151
St. George's parry, 151
Schermitore, 151
School of Musketry, Hythe, iv.
Sciabolata, 151
Scier le fer, 151
Sciogliere la misura, 151
Scorza, 171, 174
" Second Point," 2
Seconde, 40, 42, 151
—— High, 151
—— Guard, High, 151
—— line, 26
Secondo colpo, 151
Seizure, The, 151
Selmnitz, 170, 174
Selmnitz-Merjay, 171, 174
Semicircle, 151
Septime, 10, 40, 42, 151
—— line, 26
Sforzo, 151
Sgualembrato, 151
Shell, 151
Shorten Arms, 5, 17, 35, 151
Singlestick, 151
Sinner, 171, 175
Sixte, 40, 41, 152
Sixte, Centre, 87, 152
Sixte line, 26
Sixte medium, 19
Slip, To, 152
Smallsword, 152
Soie, 152
Spinazzi, 171, 175
Stjernsvard, 172, 175
Stoccata, 152
Stocken, 171, 174
Stop-thrust, 152
Stramazzone, 152

Strathnairn, Lord, 67
Strokes, 94
Stroke 1, 95
—— 2, 96
—— 3, 96
—— 4, 96
Sword, 152
'Swordsmanship,' 3, 165, 166
'Swordsmanship and Bayonet-fencing,' 54, 67, 166
Supination, 152

TAC au tac, 152
Tang, 152
Target, 152
Tempo commune, 152
Thalhofer, 172, 175
"Third Guard," 9
"Third Point," 5
Throw, 28
Thrust, 27
Tierce, 152
Tight grip, 19
Time hit, 117
Time thrust, 153
Tirer de pied ferme, 153
Tireur dangereux, 153
Tireur difficile, 153
Tireur fort, 153
Tondi, 153

Törngren, 172, 176
Touché, 153
Tour d'epée, 153
Tournament, Rl. Mil. 7, 127
Traverse, 20, 153
Tromper, 153

UN Garde d'Artillerie, 157, 174
Under-quarte, 78, 153
Under-sixte, 77, 153
Under-stop thrust, 154
Unterrichts-Plan, &c., 162
Upper inside line, 26
Upper outside line, 26

VOLTE, The, 20, 154
Volte coupe, 154
Vorschriften, Carlsruhe, 161
Vorschriften für den Unterricht, &c., Amberg, 161
Vorschriften über das B.-fechten, &c., Berlin, 161
Vorschriften für das B., Berlin, 161

WAITE, 172, 176
Weck, 172, 175
Weiss, 173, 175
Wieland, 172, 174
Woodwork of rifle, 40

www.ingramcontent.com/pod-product-compliance
Lightning Source LLC
Chambersburg PA
CBHW051055160426
43193CB00010B/1189